The Privilege for Which We Struggled

MRS ANDREAS UELAND

MRS ANSON B JACKSON

DR MABEL ULRICH

SUN FLOWER SEEDS

MRS JAMES PAIGE

MRS A H POTTER

YELLOW PAINT MRS DAVID SIMPSON

Only Yellow Flowers Will Bloom This Summer in the Yards of Suffragists

"Only yellow flowers will grow in suffragists' gardens this summer. . . . Mrs. David [Josephine] Simpson has a garden at Lake Minnetonka and here the zinnias . . . will preach their silent sermon during the hot days when no one would venture to make a real speech. Nicollet Avenue will have the benefit of a suffrage garden, for Mrs. H.G. [Elizabeth] Harrison is going to plant her flower beds at Twelfth and Nicollet with yellow flowers. Mrs. Andreas [Clara] Ueland will attend to seeing that the Lake Calhoun district is not neglected." (From the *Minneapolis Sunday Tribune*, April 4, 1915. In the Minnesota Woman Suffrage Association Records, Minnesota Historical Society)

The Privilege for Which We Struggled

Leaders of the Woman Suffrage Movement in Minnesota

Edited by
Heidi Bauer

With an Introduction by
Barbara Stuhler

UPPER MIDWEST
Women's History Center

St. Paul, Minnesota

Cover: Members of the Political Equality Club of Minneapolis marching in a suffrage parade, 1914. From the *Minneapolis Sunday Tribune*, May 3, 1914, Minnesota Historical Society.

Publication of this book was made possible, in part, with funding from the Minnesota Humanities Commission in cooperation with the National Endowment for the Humanities and the Minnesota State Legislature.

Upper Midwest Women's History Center
St. Paul 55104

Manufactured in the United States of America
10 9 8 7 6 5 4 3 2 1

International Standard Book Number 0-914-227-10-6

Photographs:

Minnesota Historical Society collections—pages 10 Bishop (Andrew Falkenshield), 16 petition (MN State Archives collection), 22 Swisshelm (museum collection), 28 Stearns (Jacoby and Bullre), 36 Ripley (museum collection), 42 Nelson (Phillips), 60 Hurd (museum collection), 66 Stockwell (*Who's Who Among Minnesota Women*), 72 Sanford (Jacoby and Son), 80 Jaeger (museum collection), 86 Simpson (museum collection), 92 Brin (Gene Garrett), 98 Schain (*Minneapolis Sunday Tribune*), 104 Colvin (B.C. Golling), 110 Ueland (Gene Garrett), 116 Francis (*Who's Who Among Minnesota Women*), 122 Harrison (*Who's Who Among Minnesota Women*), 128 Olesen (*Minneapolis Tribune*), 134 Moller (*Who's Who Among Minnesota Women*), 142 Wells (Gene Garrett), 148 Winter (museum collection), 154 Paige (museum collection), 160 Cain (museum collection)
Minneapolis Public Library, Special Collection—48 Countryman
Rhoda Gilman—54 Noyes

Library of Congress Catalog Card Number: 99-61553

*Dedicated to the women of
Minnesota who engaged in the long
struggle for the right to vote and to those
who carry on their tradition of informed
and active citizenship.*

"We have written letters, letters of protest, letters of gratitude, pleading letters, licked postage stamps, traveled miles and miles with petitions, given out thousands and thousands of sheets of literature, joined in public parades, in fact we have done all the drudgery consequent upon the forwarding of a great reform; we have done all of this year after year, month after month, day in and day out with no thought of self or fame, or recompense; we have given voluntarily and freely of our incomes, our time, our energy, asking no return save one, the granting of the privilege for which we struggled."

-Ethel Edgerton Hurd

Contents

Preface

The biographies featured in this book are of the twenty-five women whose names appear on the Minnesota Woman Suffrage Memorial on the Capitol Mall. The idea to construct the Minnesota Woman Suffrage Memorial originated with the Nineteenth Amendment Committee. The group consisted of thirty local women who convened to celebrate the seventy-fifth anniversary of the ratification of the Nineteenth Amendment to the U.S. Constitution. The committee wanted their recognition of the woman suffrage movement to extend beyond the anniversary in 1995—they wanted to create a legacy. The use of flowers to enhance a permanent monument seemed to be a logical choice, given the frequent symbolic use of flowers by the suffragists, hence the idea to design a monument incorporating a garden for the Capitol grounds was born.

The design for the memorial was chosen from among sixteen submissions in a juried competition sponsored by the Capitol Area Architectural and Planning Board. In establishing the guidelines for the competition, the use of suffrage colors—yellow/gold and white with touches of purple and green—was encouraged, and designers were given the following objectives:

    1. To honor the women of Minnesota who labored for more than fifty years in the effort to gain the right to vote.

    2. To recognize the significant accomplishments of women of Minnesota whose contributions to the well-being of the state are not represented by existing memorials.

    3. To remind visitors to the memorial of their opportunities to participate as informed and active citizens in the public life of the state.

The memorial the jury chose was "Garden of Time: Landscape of Change," designed by LOOM Architectural Firm. Once funding was secured, the groundbreaking was held in 1998 on the anniversary of the ratification of the Nineteenth Amendment—August 26, now celebrated as Women's Equality Day. Funding was provided through legislative appropriation as well as donations from individuals, foundations, and organizations. The Upper Midwest Women's History Center (UMWHC) acted as the fiscal agent for the private donations. The UMWHC also developed and published materials to enhance the memorial, including this book of biographies, curriculum packets, and brochures. These publications will serve the general public as well as students seeking to learn more about the woman suffrage movement and the Minnesota women who kept the fight alive.

The women featured on the memorial, and whose biographies appear in this book, were chosen for their contributions to the Minnesota suffrage movement with the following criteria in mind: They are all Minnesota women, if not by birth then by contribution, they are no longer living, and their work on behalf of suffrage and other causes was a significant part of their lives. Special attention was given to creating a diverse list of women. Although the majority of the women involved in the movement were upper-class white women from Minneapolis and St. Paul, a little additional research reveals that other women from different backgrounds also made contributions to the cause and so are included in these pages.

While the accomplishments of these women are especially significant, they are only a small cross section of the countless women—and men—who made the victory of woman suffrage a reality. The woman suffrage movement attracted people from all walks of life and united them in a way that no other cause or measure had previously done.

The biographies as they appear in this book are arranged chronologically based on involvement in the suffrage movement. They have also been grouped into four categories, designed to reflect the changing face and activity of the suffrage movement in Minnesota as well as on a national level.

Through their passionate work for woman suffrage, the Minnesota women featured in this volume won for future generations of women the right to vote. We are left with the responsibility to educate ourselves and others in order to fully participate in the betterment of our society.

Heidi Bauer
1999

Acknowledgments

This book would not have been possible without the considerable dedication, talent, and knowledge of Upper Midwest Women's History Center Director Susan Hill Gross and Associate Director Sheila Ahlbrand. Each spent countless hours editing, researching, and brainstorming with me. In addition, their encouragement and support helped me develop this project into something that I am proud of.

I am also grateful for the talents of Barbara Stuhler, who served as the historical consultant for this project. She has more knowledge of woman suffrage in Minnesota than any reference book, and was always willing to lend her expertise. The staff at the Minnesota Historical Society Research Center, particularly Ron Walruth, was also helpful and ready to offer assistance.

Of course all the gifted scholars who contributed biographies to this work deserve countless thanks as well. They each captured the spirit of the woman they wrote about and made her come alive to be a source of inspiration.

Thanks and praise go to Julie Michener, our desktop publisher. From helping us through computer woes to producing the layout, she has been indispensable to this project.

The Nineteenth Amendment Committee and the Capitol Area Architectural and Planning Board deserve recognition for developing the Minnesota Woman Suffrage Memorial. Without that original project, these biographies would not have been written.

Finally I would like to thank my family and friends, including my parents, Nancy and Randy, April McHugh, Jennifer Thorson, and especially Jason Clapp. They listened enthusiastically, offered suggestions, helped me keep my sense of humor, and provided continuous support throughout this project.

Introduction

by Barbara Stuhler

More than two centuries ago the Declaration of Independence extolled the equality of men and assigned to them— but not to women—certain inalienable rights. From that time onward, individual women protested this partial citizenship, but their protests did not bear fruit for nearly a century and a half, when they finally won the right to vote with the ratification of the Nineteenth Amendment in 1920.

The campaign for woman suffrage began in the United States in 1848 when a group of five women, led by Lucretia Mott and Elizabeth Cady Stanton, called the first woman's rights convention in Seneca Falls, New York. The most contentious debate centered on a resolution stating that "it is the duty of the women of this country to secure themselves their sacred right to the elective franchise." Seventy-two years later, women gained voices and votes in the government structure under whose laws they were obliged to live.

The fundamental reason for denying women the vote was the presumption that politics was not their work. The demand for the vote subverted the widely held notion that a woman's place was in the home; it fell to men to bear the burden of the public domain, a burden that many men (and some women) thought inappropriate for women. People of this persuasion feared that suffrage would replace male authority with female autonomy, change women's role within the family structure from subordinate to equal, and open the door for women to move from the domestic sphere into the public arena.

In addition to these anxieties about gender roles, other political concerns prompted male decision makers (and men in general) to oppose suffrage. Despite the reassurances of southern women to the contrary, lawmakers in the South feared that suffrage would jeopardize white supremacy. In eastern states such as Massachusetts, the male hierarchy of the Catholic Church was against woman suffrage and actively led the opposition. In midwestern states such as Minnesota and Wisconsin, where brewers and liquor interests occupied a preeminent economic position, "wets" (those against the prohibition of alcohol) feared the temperance inclinations of women.

Even though the Seneca Falls convention marked the beginning of the woman suffrage movement, women did not form their own suffrage organizations until 1869, when the Fourteenth Amendment enfranchised African American men but excluded women. Disagreements over what abolitionist Wendell Phillips called the "Negro's hour" severed the abolitionist/suffragist alliance. Women who had relied on antislavery groups to support woman suffrage now had to promote their own cause. More accepting of the "Negro's hour," Lucy Stone and her husband, Henry Blackwell, formed the American Woman Suffrage Association. Angry about women's exclusion, Susan B. Anthony and Elizabeth Cady Stanton created the more militant National Woman Suffrage Association. The passage of time and influence of younger suffragists brought about the merger in 1890 of the two groups into the National American Woman Suffrage Association (NAWSA).

The woman suffrage movement was formally introduced in Minnesota in the 1860s when the legislature was besieged with petitions from disparate "friends of equality" groups who pressed for the enfranchisement of women. On one occasion in 1868, when a recommendation "to amend the constitution by striking out the word 'male' as a requisite for voting or holding office" reached the floor of the Minnesota House of Representatives, it was greeted with laughter and quickly tabled. Such was the mind-set of Minnesota legislators. By 1875, however, male voters approved a constitutional amendment enacted by the legislature giving women the right to vote in school elections. Two years later, male voters turned down an amendment allowing women to vote on the "whiskey question." In session after session, Minnesota legislators defeated efforts to extend voting rights either to taxpaying women or to all women in municipal elections and on temperance issues.

An organized effort on behalf of woman suffrage developed in Minnesota in 1869 when Sarah Burger Stearns and Mary Jackman Colburn formed independent suffrage societies in Rochester and Champlin. Other local organizations also sprang up, mostly in the southeastern area of the state. Not until 1881 did fourteen women—including Harriet Bishop, Stearns, and Julia Bullard Nelson—meet in Hastings to establish the Minnesota Woman Suffrage Association (MWSA). Stearns was elected as the first president of the MWSA. The group's membership grew to 124 in the first year and doubled in the second, probably representing individuals living in communities without local societies. The MWSA's strategy was to increase its membership and influence by sustaining existing societies and establishing new auxiliaries. These auxiliaries deferred to the MWSA for leadership at the legislature and responded as requested with letters, petitions, and attendance at gatherings.

Exemplifying the tactics and experiencing the frustration of the movement's early years, pioneer leaders such as Stearns also bore the brunt of public outrage, rejection, and ridicule that was especially intense in this inaugural period. Only one of these early leaders, Ethel Edgerton Hurd, lived to see the day of victory.

By the early 1900s, organizational efforts proved to be more effective both in Minnesota and on the national level. For one thing, traveling and communication had become easier. Women had also acquired education and experience through the study groups and women's clubs that flourished after the American Civil War. More worldly and informed, they had learned how to manage organizations. (Lucretia Mott's husband, James, had presided at the landmark Seneca

Falls convention because women simply had no experience running meetings.) As the movement progressed into the twentieth century, second-generation suffragists across the country stood determined to bring the campaign to a successful conclusion.

Despite this enthusiasm, the movement hit a lull. In 1914, a group of young suffragists, chafing at the slow pace of progress, took charge of the NAWSA's inactive congressional committee and brought it to life with daring initiatives such as parades, street speaking, and other noisy and notable activities. Uneasy with each other's company, the two NAWSA factions split, with the younger women departing to form the Congressional Union for Woman Suffrage. In 1916 the same group of young leaders formed the Woman's Party to represent female voters in the twelve enfranchised states. A year later the party and the Congressional Union came together as the National Woman's Party (NWP).

The NWP broke with suffrage tradition by engaging in partisan politics. The group's strategy was to campaign against the party in power—if those holding elected office had not yet granted woman suffrage, maybe a new person would. The NWP campaigned against all Democratic candidates in suffrage states and picketed the White House and the Capitol to protest the continuing refusal by the president and the Congress to recognize women's right to vote. Such unconventional behavior seemed counterproductive to NAWSA leaders, who were trying to win the approval and votes of decision makers.

The NWP picketers were arrested following their protests, and were sentenced to jail or workhouses. While incarcerated, some of the women were starved, beaten, placed in solitary confinement, and forcibly fed following organized hunger strikes to protest their poor treatment. The struggles and mistreatment of these women in prison began to receive a great deal of attention, and public sympathy swung their way. Those who served sentences received NWP prison pins fashioned as badges of honor for having been "jailed for freedom," a phrase coined by Doris Stevens in her book of the same name.

The division between the NAWSA and the NWP represented a classic case of disagreement over the most effective means to accomplish a common purpose. In this case, however, division proved to be not weakness but strength. The NAWSA and its state affiliates provided political organization and pressure, and their contributions on the home front during World War I (working for the Red Cross, promoting food conservation, and the like) helped to win the support of President Wilson and sway public opinion to their side. Although there were moments when relations between the two organizations were strained over tactics and claims for primacy, both parties realized, as Minnesota suffrage leader Clara Ueland once wrote, "The main thing, and really the only thing, is that the work is nearly finished."

It was Clara Ueland who directed the final act of the suffrage movement in Minnesota as the last president of the Minnesota Woman Suffrage Association. Like women leaders in other states who had acquired education and experience in making things happen, she was an articulate spokeswoman whose style was more organized than charismatic.

What a difference a leader can make! Following a succession of four presidents in four years and the organizational disarray suggested by that turnover, Ueland came to office with a considered set of priorities. Her goals were to hire and support an efficient organizer, to magnify the association's clout by organizing in political districts, and to assign specific responsibilities to each board member. She was determined to improve the operations of the MWSA and to transform the suffrage organizations throughout the state into highly sophisticated mechanisms of persuasion, pressure, and action. In the five years of her presidency, she achieved her original objectives and more. By 1919, some 30,000 Minnesota women had taken a stand for suffrage by joining various local societies. Consequently, it was no surprise that the state legislature finally enacted presidential suffrage for women in 1919. A year later in a special session, Minnesota became the fifteenth state to ratify the Nineteenth Amendment to the U.S. Constitution, which became law on August 26, 1920.

-Originally published in a different format in
Minnesota History *54 (Fall 1995).*

Buelcher, Steve M. *Women's Movements in the United States: Woman Suffrage, Equal Rights, and Beyond.* New Brunswick, N.J.: Rutgers University Press, 1990.

DuBois, Ellen C. *Feminism and Suffrage: The Emergence of an Independent Women's Movement in America, 1848-1869.* Ithaca: Cornell University Press, 1978.

Flexner, Eleanor. *Century of Struggle: The Woman's Rights Movement in the United States.* Cambridge: Belknap Press of Harvard University Press, 1959.

Irwin, Inez Haynes. *The Story of the Woman's Party.* New York: Harcourt, Brace and Co., 1921.

Kraditor, Aileen S. *The Ideas of the Woman Suffrage Movement, 1890-1920.* Garden City, N.Y.: Doubleday & Company, 1971.

Martin, Theodora P. *The Sound of Our Own Voices: Women's Study Clubs, 1860-1910.* Boston: Beacon Press, 1987.

Minnesota. House of Representatives. *Journal*, 1868, 1875.

___ Secretary of State. *Legislative Manual*, 1885-86.

___ Senate. *Journal*, 1875, 1877.

Minnesota Woman Suffrage Association Records (microfilm edition), Minnesota Historical Society.

St. Paul Pioneer Press, 24 January 1868.

Scott, Anne Firor and Andrew MacKay Scott. *One Half the People: The Fight for Woman Suffrage.* Philadelphia: Lippincott, 1975. Reprint. Urbana: University of Illinois Press, 1982.

Stanton, Elizabeth Cady, et. al. *History of Woman Suffrage.* Vol. 3. Rochester, N.Y.: Susan B. Anthony, 1886.

Stuhler, Barbara. *Gentle Warriors: Clara Ueland and the Minnesota Struggle for Woman Suffrage.* St. Paul: Minnesota Historical Society Press, 1995.

Swisshelm, Jane Grey. *Crusader and Feminist: Letters of Jane Grey Swisshelm, 1858-1865.* Edited by Arthur L. Larsen. St. Paul: Minnesota Historical Society, 1934.

Trailblazers

Harriet Bishop

(1818-1883)

by Norma Sommerdorf

Man may bid the tall forest tree to bow; he may make the waste places smile with plenty; he may engage in political strife, and his eloquence thrill the nation; or he may hold the scepter of power: but to woman a higher, a nobler work is entrusted. It is her province to train the tender twig and to mold the plastic clay. Upon her it depends, whether the individual American citizen shall be a curse or a blessing, and whether the nation shall be rent and prostrated by the feuds of corrupt men, or fulfill the mission of the great Christian republic of modern times.

- Harriet Bishop in *Floral Home or First Years in Minnesota*

When individuals signed on to become charter members of the Minnesota Woman Suffrage Association in 1881, Harriet Bishop's name was at the top of the list. Her years of training St. Paul's children and organizing in the community, as well as personal disappointments, brought her to this position. It proved to be quite a journey, considering that when she arrived in Minnesota thirty-four years earlier she had just finished a course taught by Catharine Beecher, who proclaimed that women could be a stronger influence without the vote by acting through more traditional roles. Her life experiences taught Harriet that women could not depend on husbands or children to vote their will, and when the opportunity came to help organize for woman suffrage, she signed on.

Harriet Bishop advocated for children and their welfare all her life. Born in Panton, Vermont, she determined at an early age to dedicate herself to teaching and organizing for change. After completing her training, she taught in various Essex County, New York, schools, a short ferry ride across Lake Champlain from her home.

Bishop had been a teacher for about ten years when she heard of the National Board of Popular Education's plan to send teachers to western settlements, where children were growing up in isolated areas without an education. Founded by Catharine Beecher, sister of *Uncle Tom's Cabin* author Harriet Beecher Stowe, this group provided a training session in Albany, New York, which Bishop attended. A letter read to the class described St. Paul as a village with five stores, all of which sold intoxicating drinks. More than half the parents of the students would be unable to read, and the teacher should expect students who were English, French, Swiss, Chippewa, Sioux, and African. Bishop was the first of the class to volunteer, and became the first teacher this organization sent "to the West." She is recognized as Minnesota's first public school teacher.

Traveling an involved river route, Bishop arrived in St. Paul to begin work in 1847. The building made available for the schoolhouse was an abandoned blacksmith shop, but she and the students gathered pine boughs to hang on the walls to freshen the interior. Following the first week of school she invited the children to come back on Sunday, thus starting the first interdenominational Sunday School in Minnesota.

Within months she organized the St. Paul Circle of Industry to raise funds to build a new school. By the time the building was finished a year later, it had already outgrown its several purposes of school, courtroom, lecture hall, church, and polling place envisioned by the women who planned it because thousands of new residents began to arrive after the Minnesota Territory was established in 1849.

Bishop was an able organizer and looked to by residents of the village for leadership. She gathered people together to form many early St. Paul organizations. The new school building served as a site for the formation of the Sons of Temperance, formed to address the visible problem of drunkenness. Bishop enlisted many former students to sign a pledge of abstinence during the years to come.

Bishop was also an author and a promoter. *Floral Home or First Years of Minnesota*, recording her impressions and the history of her early years in the state, was published in 1857. Later, she collected material for *Dakota War Whoop or Indian Massacres and War in Minnesota of 1862-3*. She published a book-length poem, *Minnesota: Then and Now* in 1869 and several other poems in *The Poets and Poetry of Minnesota*, published in 1864. She made numerous trips east, representing investors who wanted to buy land in St. Paul.

In 1858, she married John McConkey, a widower with four children, and raised his children during the years he served in the Civil War. The unhappy marriage was ended in 1867, and Harriet requested the Minnesota legislature to restore her maiden name, after which she was known as Mrs. Harriet Bishop.

In 1867 she helped organize the Ladies Christian Union which established the "Home for the Friendless," (now Wilder Residence East). When it first opened, the building was a shelter for women and children, a home for orphans, and a residence for elderly women. The Philecclesian Literary Society, a reading and discussion group, was initiated in her home, and she traveled throughout the state organizing new chapters for the Women's Christian Temperance Union. At the charter meeting of the group, she argued that "the work should be done by women in women's way," and warned against the appointment of "men who wish to enlist under our banner."

Harriet Bishop championed the cause of prohibition and of the vote for women until her death in 1883, but did not live to see these measures become law in the Eighteenth and Nineteenth Amendments to the U.S. Constitution.

Bishop, Harriet E. *Floral Home or First Years in Minnesota*. New York: Sheldon, Blakeman and Co., 1857.

Kaufman, Polly Welt. *Women Teachers on the Frontier*. New Haven: Yale University Press, 1984.

Williams, J. Fletcher. *The History of the City of St. Paul to 1875*. 1876. Reprint, St. Paul: Minnesota Historical Society, 1983.

Yesteryears with the W.C.T.U. Compiled by the Women's Christian Temperance Union. Copy in Minnesota Historical Society.

THE FRANCHISE FOR WOMEN.

PETITION.

1889

To the Senate and House of Representatives of the State of Minnesota in Legislature Assembled:

We, the undersigned, inhabitants of the State of Minnesota, respectfully petition your honorable body to take measures for amending our State Constitution, by striking out the word "male," as a requisite qualification for voting or holding office.

A photograph of Mary Jackman Colburn could not be located;
her name is the third from the top on the left

16

Mary Jackman Colburn
(1811-1901)

---

by Lynn McCarthy

*I will not stoop longer to ask of any congress or legisla-
ture for that which I know to be mine.*

> - Mary Jackman Colburn, in a letter to a friend
> after winning a Minnesota legislature-sponsored
> essay contest in 1864

Pioneer, trailblazer, vanguard, forerunner, precursor. All these words embody the indomitable spirit of Mary Jackman Colburn. From the beginning she plunged into territories previously uncharted by women. Her strong personality and righteous indignation drove her to fight for woman's rights when at the time doing so was considered by many to be, at best, hopeless and, at worst, "unwomanly" and morally wrong.

Mary Jackman was born in October, 1811, in Newburyport, Massachusetts. In the 1840s, Mary asserted her independence and left home to study medicine. She faced a prejudice voiced by students of Harvard Medical School who actually passed the following resolution in 1850:

> 1) . . . no woman of true delicacy would be
> willing in the presence of men to listen to the
> discussions of the subjects that necessarily

come under consideration of the student of medicine and 2) that we object to having the company of any female forced upon us, who is disposed to unsex herself, and to sacrifice her modesty by appearing with men in the lecture room.

Undaunted, Mary studied and later graduated with a medical degree. During her studies, she met Samuel Colburn, an ambitious man who matched her pioneering spirit. His humble beginnings as a baker belied his ambition, which drove him to become a strong and prominent civic leader. They married in 1844 in Hopedale, Massachusetts. In the true spirit of pioneering, Mary and Samuel moved to Moline, Illinois in 1849, a town incorporated only the year before. There she again flouted convention and put her medical training to use by practicing medicine for five years.

In 1854, the Colburn's moved even farther west into the vast wilderness of the newly established Minnesota Territory. They settled on a parcel of land bisected by Elm Creek in what was soon to become the city of Champlin, Minnesota. Samuel was one of the three founding fathers of Champlin and later served, among other things, as justice of the peace, postmaster, town clerk, assessor, and auditor.

Mary, too, made an indelible mark on the community. In 1858, as Minnesota celebrated its statehood, she celebrated and defended women by giving what was probably the first public lecture in Minnesota on woman's rights, titled "The Rights and Wrongs of Women" at her home in Champlin. In 1864, Colburn entered a statewide contest sponsored by the Minnesota legislature which offered prizes for the two best essays "setting forth the advantages which this State [Minnesota] offers to immigrants, and giving useful information with regard to the State." The prizes were awarded by a committee of six men appointed by the governor—Colburn won the $200 first prize. In his congratulatory letter, the Commissioner of Immigration, D. Blakely, obviously expecting the winner to be a man, referred to M. J. Colburn as "sir."

Colburn's prize-winning essay was published and widely circulated. Later, it was translated into Swedish and a second English edition was published.

Perhaps it was the offensive assumption that only a man could win such a contest that reignited Colburn's zeal, for not long after winning the contest she resumed her fight for woman's rights with a vengeance. In January 1867, she joined forces with Sarah Burger Stearns, a formidable suffragist in her own right, and with the assistance of A. J. Spaulding, editor of the *Anoka Star,* requested a hearing before the legislature. At the request of Colburn and several other parties, Representative John Seboski presented a petition signed by 200 men and women "praying for the extension of the right of suffrage to females." It was referred to a special committee. In February, Mary Colburn and Sarah Stearns were invited to address the House on "the subject of female suffrage." In absentia, Stearns sent a letter to Representative Seboski which was duly read and printed. After much communication back and forth, Colburn was granted the right to address the legislature. Unfortunately, due to miscommunication about the actual lecture time, she missed her first appointment but was granted a time to speak later only out of the "gentlemanly courtesy" of the legislature.

As trying as Colburn's first experience with the legislature must have been, neither it, nor the defeat of a bill in 1868 which called for an amendment to the Minnesota Constitution striking out the word "male" as a constitutional qualification for voting, slowed her efforts. In 1869, she organized one of the first local suffrage societies in Minnesota in her home town of Champlin.

In 1884, after forty years of marriage, Samuel died. Near the end of her life Mary Colburn became an invalid and though nearly blind and deaf, she retained her faculties and cheerfulness to the last "repeating poetry and prose for the entertainment of her hearers with a spirit of intelligence and understanding." She died in 1901 at the age of ninety. Though she never saw the Nineteenth Amendment ratified, it was the enthusiastic and tireless work of Colburn and others like her that brought Minnesota women another step closer to gaining social, political and economic freedom.

Anoka Herald, 27 December 1901.

Braude, Ann. *Radical Spirits: Spiritualism and Women's Rights in Nineteenth Century America*. Boston: Beacon Press, 1989.

Colburn, Mary. In *Minnesota as a Home for Immigrants*. St. Paul: Minnesota State Board of Immigration, 1865.

Journal of the House of Representatives of the Ninth Session of the Legislature of the State of Minnesota. St. Paul: The House of Representatives, 1867.

Marks, Geoffrey, and William K. Beatty. *Women in White*. New York: Charles Scribner's Sons, 1972.

Miller, Orange. *History of Champlin, Minnesota*. Anoka, Minn.: Pease Printery Press, 1936.

Stanton, Elizabeth Cady, et al. *History of Woman Suffrage*, 6 vols. Rochester, NY: Susan B. Anthony; New York: National American Woman Suffrage Association, 1881-1922.

Stephens, Ruth, et al. *Champlin on the Mississippi*. Champlin, Minn: Champlin Bicentennial Historical Projects, Inc., 1979.

Jane Grey Swisshelm
(1815-1884)

by Sheila Ahlbrand

Women should not weaken their cause by impracticable demands. Make no claim which could not be won in a reasonable time. Take one step at a time, get a good foothold in it and advance carefully.

- Jane Grey Swisshelm in *Half a Century*, concerning the *Pittsburgh Saturday Visiter*'s [*sic*] policy in regard to woman's rights

Jane Grey Swisshelm was a gradualist. She believed that woman's rights, including suffrage, should be won slowly, one fight at a time. An independent woman, Swisshelm was often unkind to the suffrage movement even though she believed in the cause. She always believed her own way was the best, and never joined a suffrage association. When she came to Minnesota in June of 1857 she was already one of the most famous and controversial women in the United States, and though she lived here for less than a decade, she left an indelible mark on the state's history. Using wit and sarcasm as her tools, she regularly voiced her opinions about abolition, woman's rights and suffrage in the various newspapers she wrote for throughout her life. Perhaps more famous as an abolitionist, Swisshelm's personal experience made her a passionate advocate of woman's rights, often drawing parallels between the condition of a slave and a wife.

Pittsburgh, Pennsylvania, was still a frontier town when Jane Grey Cannon was born there in 1815 into a strict Presbyterian family. Jane was a precocious child, and by age three had learned to read the Bible and recite the catechism. Her father died in 1823, leaving her mother with three young children to support. All of the children worked to help make money, and Jane learned lace making and painting. Later, she was sent to boarding school for a short time, and when her mother could no longer afford to send her the director offered her board and tuition in exchange for teaching the younger girls.

Despite her father's death when she was young, Jane's early life had been pleasant. But that was to change in 1836 when she married James Swisshelm, a dashing young farmer who had rescued her and her schoolmates from a wagon accident when she was in boarding school. Their marriage was unhappy from the start. The first few months of marriage she lived with her mother, and he lived with his. He convinced Jane to give up reading everything except the Bible, and her own sense of duty to her husband convinced her to give up painting, which she had grown to love.

In 1838 the couple moved to Louisville, Kentucky. It was here that Swisshelm, upon witnessing the cruelties of slavery firsthand, became a staunch abolitionist. It was also here that she began to compare the condition of a slave with that of a wife. Business had not gone well for James in Louisville, and they were largely supported by the corset-making business Swisshelm had started. However, in 1839 Swisshelm returned to Pittsburgh to care for her dying mother. When Swisshelm's mother died in 1840, James threatened to sue her estate for the value of his wife's nursing services. Swisshelm was appalled to learn that the law gave her husband, as owner of her person and property, the right to do so.

Jane Swisshelm remained in Pennsylvania, where she began teaching again, while her husband stayed in Kentucky.

It was during this time that she began writing. When she and her husband reunited in 1842, he, who had encouraged his wife to stop reading, supported her writing career because of the money it brought to the family. Swisshelm began by writing for local papers. She was a correspondent for the *Pittsburgh Commercial Journal*, to which she wrote a series of letters on married women's property rights. Due in part to this work, the Pennsylvania legislature, in the 1847-48 session, gave married women the right to hold property. This same year, 1848, Swisshelm began her own abolitionist newspaper, the *Pittsburgh Saturday Visiter* [*sic*]. The paper was successful, and eventually had a national circulation of 6,000.

Although Swisshelm's writing inspired women to stand up for their rights, she didn't always approve of the results. In the summer of 1849 she received a letter from a woman in Salem, Ohio, stating that the *Visiter* "had stirred up so much interest in woman's rights that a meeting had been held and a committee appointed to get up a woman's rights convention." She then asked Swisshelm if she would preside over the convention. Swisshelm declined, and asked the women to reconsider having the convention. She told the women in Salem she was afraid that a convention would "open a door through which fools and fanatics [would] pour in, and make the cause ridiculous."

Despite her success as a writer, and the birth of a daughter in 1851, Jane Swisshelm's marriage had become intolerable, and in 1857 she left her husband and took her young daughter with her to Minnesota. She planned on leading a quiet, retiring life there, but that didn't last for long. A short time after her arrival she became the editor of the *St. Cloud Visiter* [*sic*], and began a contest of wills with a federal officer named Sylvanus Lowry, who practically ran the upper half of the Minnesota territory. The *St. Cloud Visiter* was dependent on financial backers, and Lowry promised to support the *Visiter* if Swisshelm would endorse President James Buchanan. To his surprise Swisshelm agreed. However, her first article in support of Buchanan was a biting satire, naming all the qualities she found most disagreeable about the politician as reasons for her endorsement.

What ensued was all out war. Insults in the form of mock praise were volleyed back and forth, until one insult became too personal, and Lowry and two other men broke in and destroyed the *Visiter's* printing press. In her first public speech, Swisshelm gave her account of the events, and, with public support, new printing equipment was rushed in from Chicago. In the next issue of the *Visiter* she named the men who broke into her offices, upon which Lowry promptly sued the paper for libel. To protect the other backers of the *Visiter*, Swisshelm printed a formal apology to Lowry in what would be the last issue of the paper. The following day she started the *St. Cloud Democrat*, with herself as sole owner, and picked up where the *Visiter* left off.

In her first public speech defending herself against the attack by Lowry, Swisshelm discovered she was a good speaker. Subsequently, she became a popular lecturer both in Minnesota and elsewhere. In 1863 she traveled east, and although she continued as a correspondent for the *Democrat* she did not return to Minnesota. After leaving Minnesota she served as a Civil War nurse, started another newspaper, and in 1872 went on a lecture tour through Illinois speaking on woman's suffrage. She died in Pennsylvania at the age of sixty-eight.

Luther, Sally. "Journalist Jane Swisshelm: She Made Her Readers Roar," *Minneapolis Sunday Tribune*, 28 August 1949.

McCarthy, Abigail. "Jane Grey Swisshelm: Marriage and Slavery," In Barbara Stuhler and Gretchen Kreuter, eds, *Women of Minnesota: Selected Biographical Essays*. St. Paul: Minnesota Historical Society Press, 1977, 1998 revised.

Meier, Peg. "Where Jane Grey Swisshelm Made One of Her Many Stands," *Minneapolis Star Tribune*, 3 March 1997.

Stanton, Elizabeth Cady, et al. *History of Woman Suffrage*. Vol. 3. Rochester, N.Y.: Susan B. Anthony, 1885.

Swisshelm, Jane Grey. *Crusader and Feminist; Letters of Jane Grey Swisshelm*. Edited and with an introduction and notes by Arthur J. Larsen. St. Paul: Minnesota Historical Society Press, 1934.

Swisshelm, Jane Grey. *Half a Century*. 1880. New York: Source Book Press, 1970.

Tyler, Alice Felt. *Notable American Women 1607-1950: A Biographical Dictionary*. Vol. 3. Edited by Edward T. James. Cambridge: Belknap Press of Harvard University Press, 1971.

Weatherford, Doris. *American Women's History: An A to Z of People, Organizations, Issues, and Events*. New York: Prentice Hall General Reference, 1994.

Sarah Burger Stearns
(1836-1904)

by Norma Sommerdorf and Sheila Ahlbrand

The advocates of suffrage in Minnesota were so few in the early days, and their homes so remote from each other, that there was little chance for cooperation, hence the history of the movement in this State consists more of personal efforts than of conventions, legislative hearings and judicial decisions.

> - Sarah Burger Stearns in *History of Woman Suffrage, Volume Three*

Sarah Burger Stearns began her work for woman's rights when she was only fourteen years old, and continued this work for the rest of her life. Born in New York City in 1836, she moved with her parents to Ann Arbor, Michigan, in 1845. It was in Michigan where she truly began her career as an advocate. As editor of her school paper, she noted the injustice of the exclusion of women from the state university. Two years later, at age sixteen, she attended a suffrage convention in Ohio, where she was inspired by speeches from such famous suffrage leaders as Lucretia Mott and Lucy Stone. By the time she was in her early twenties she had started to turn her ideas into actions.

In 1858, Stearns and twelve other young women petitioned the University of Michigan at Ann Arbor to admit women. Although this attempt was unsuccessful, it did pave the way for women to be admitted eleven years later. Stearns went to the State Normal School in Ypsilanti, Michigan, and became a teacher after completing her education. In 1863 she married attorney Ozora Stearns who, ironically, graduated from the very university that refused to admit her. He was in the service and was sent to the front lines of the Civil War shortly after they were married. While he was away, Stearns moved back to her hometown in Michigan. When Ozora Stearns was relieved of his duties after the war ended, the couple moved to Rochester, Minnesota in 1866.

That same year, at a local Fourth of July celebration, Sarah Stearns was asked to speak on the topic, "Our young and growing state; may she ever be an honor to her citizens." She took this opportunity to give a speech on woman suffrage, which was received with cheers. The next year, Stearns, along with Mary Jackman Colburn, was granted a special hearing before the legislature to petition for an amendment striking the word "male" from the Minnesota Constitution, which granted the vote to "every male person." However, in 1868, when a bill was introduced proposing the desired amendment, it was defeated. Undaunted, Stearns continued her work, and in 1869 started the first woman's suffrage society in her home in Rochester.

In the spring of 1872, the Stearns' moved to Duluth where Ozora Stearns became a District Court Judge. During their years in Duluth Sarah was elected to the Duluth Board of Education, founded a state shelter for women and children "needing self-help and self-protection," and began the Duluth Woman Suffrage Circle.

When the Minnesota Woman Suffrage Association (MWSA) was formed in 1881, it was no surprise that Stearns was elected as its first president. One newspaper reported that Stearns, "possessed the tenacity of purpose, the dogged persistence of the true reformer; no discouragements, rebuffs nor ingratitude seemed to dishearten her or swerve her from what she considered right." In the first year 124 members were enrolled in the MWSA, and during the second year that number more than doubled.

Like many suffragists, Stearns was also involved in the temperance movement, serving as the recording secretary and chair of the resolutions committee for the first Woman's Christian Temperance Union state convention in 1878. Stearns chaired the first session of the convention, at which it was decided that women did not need to form a separate political party:

> Resolved, that while the strong conviction of our hearts is that because of this destroyer in our homes the prohibition of the liquor traffic is demanded by the people of Minnesota, we, as a Christian Temperance Union, do not propose to indicate to the voters of the state by what way or through what political organizations prohibition shall be secured.

By 1883, health problems compelled Stearns to abdicate her leadership in the suffrage movement to others, but this setback would not keep her down for long. At the 1884 annual state suffrage meeting, held in Minneapolis, she gave a speech on "the new era to be inaugurated when women have the ballot," and around 1885 she accepted the position of president of the Equal Rights League in Duluth. She also wrote the chapter on Minnesota for the third volume of *The History of Woman Suffrage* compiled by Elizabeth Cady Stanton, Susan B. Anthony, and Matilda Joslyn Gage.

Stearns continued her work in Minnesota, and her speeches at the annual suffrage meetings generated a lot of attention. In 1892, at the annual meeting of the MWSA in Hastings, Minnesota, she read a letter from Susan B. Anthony, while her speech at the annual meeting in Lake City, Minnesota, in 1893, focused not only on woman suffrage, but also on dress reform.

Unfortunately, her husband became ill, compelling the couple to move to the warmer climate of California in 1895, but they returned for the summers to the family home in Duluth. Stearns died suddenly at her California home in January of 1904. She had energetically followed the ideals of her youth throughout her life, remaining an active member of the Los Angeles Suffrage League up to the time of her death.

"The Suffrage Association." *The Daily Gazette*, 9 September 1892.

Duluth News Tribune, 26 January 1904.

"A Grand Success," *Graphic Sentinel*, 29 August, 1893.

Livermore, Mary A. and Frances Willard. *Woman of the Century*. Detroit: Gale Research, Inc., 1974.

Stanton, Elizabeth Cady, et. al. *History of Woman Suffrage*. Vol. 3. Rochester, N.Y.: Susan B. Anthony, 1885.

Continuing the
Struggle

Martha Rogers Ripley
(1843-1912)

by Rhoda Gilman

Is everything all right at the hospital?

- Last words of Dr. Martha Rogers Ripley

In 1886, Minneapolis, like most cities in the country, had no hospital that would admit an unwed mother for childbirth or other medical care. Such a woman deserved nothing, it was thought, but disgrace and punishment. Dr. Martha Ripley disagreed. Three years earlier she had become one of only eight female physicians in the city, and her practice was heavily weighted toward obstetrics. Faced with three unmarried patients who were desperately in need of care, she rented a small house and hired a nurse. It was the beginning of Maternity Hospital, which in time became one of the most distinguished medical facilities in the Midwest for care of mothers and newborn children.

Martha George Rogers had not dreamed of being a doctor when she was growing up on the prairies of northeastern Iowa, although as a patriotic teenager during the Civil War, she did try to become an army nurse. She had been only four years old when her family moved from Vermont in 1847 to a pioneer farm on the Little Turkey River, close to Fort Atkinson, Iowa. She returned to New England again after her marriage in 1867 to William Ripley, scion of a Massachusetts mill-owning family.

Ripley's first years in Massachusetts were taken up with the birth of three daughters and charitable work among the families of mill workers, but by 1875 she was deeply involved in the movement for woman suffrage. She became a close friend of Lucy Stone and Henry Blackwell, who were making Boston a hotbed of political work for woman's rights. In 1876 she began six years as a member of the state central committee of the Massachusetts Woman Suffrage Association. An outspoken debater and fine public speaker, Ripley was in demand throughout the state, and she came to know many professional women, including several doctors.

It was in 1880 that she enrolled at the Boston University School of Medicine. This placed her in the homeopathic tradition, which the school taught and which throughout the nineteenth century was more open to women than was regular allopathic medicine. Before her graduation with honors in 1883, William Ripley was disabled by a mill accident and forced to retire from business. Thus the new doctor unexpectedly faced becoming the main support of the family. Friends and relatives in Minneapolis urged her to open a practice in the Midwestern mill town. Although discouraged at first, she decided to relocate, even though she would "not say that she likes it better than Boston."

Minnesota reached out to Ripley, however. Even before her family was permanently settled there, she was elected president of the Minnesota Woman Suffrage Association. Because of her prominence and many acquaintances in the movement, she was able to bring the national convention of the American Woman Suffrage Association to Minneapolis in 1885. This as well as an alliance she made with the temperance forces in the state gave a much-needed lift to the struggling Minnesota suffrage organization.

Within six years Dr. Ripley's growing medical practice and her tireless lobbying of legislators to improve the legal rights and health of women took her away from active leadership in the cause of suffrage. Denial of the right to vote was just one aspect of the discrimination faced by Minnesota women. Until 1891 the age of consent was only ten years old, causing Ripley to note, in one of many blistering letters she sent to Minneapolis editors, that the property of young girls was better protected by the state than their persons. In another letter she declared that a law adopted by the legislature in 1889 that empowered fathers to will away their unborn children was "worthy of the Dark Ages."

Ripley soon became one of the city's most vocal reformers—frequently ridiculed, but widely respected. Absence of matrons on the Minneapolis police force and of women on the city's school board were causes upon which she spoke out vigorously. As a medical person she was also dedicated to promotion of sanitation and public health, including the then radical concept of cremation.

But it was in the creation of Maternity Hospital that Ripley made her greatest impact on Minneapolis and the Midwest. From its small beginnings in 1886 it quickly grew to occupy a permanent twenty-room facility and became a corporation formed "to provide a lying-in hospital" both for married women without means of adequate care and for "girls who have previously borne a good character" but "have been led astray." It also undertook to "care for destitute children born in this institution." In 1896 the hospital moved to its final location at the corner of Western and Penn Avenue North, where it achieved one of the lowest maternal death rates in the region and became the first Minneapolis hospital to establish a social service department.

Although the cause of suffrage moved from the forefront of Martha Ripley's life, her devotion to it never ceased. By the turn of the century she had become a bridge between the earliest pioneers of the struggle and the new generation of younger women who would live to see its final success. Older leaders like Frances Willard and new ones like Carrie Chapman Catt were equally welcome as guests in the Ripleys' hospitable Minneapolis home.

When Martha Ripley died in 1912 plans were already under way for a new building on the site of Maternity Hospital. In 1915 it was dedicated as the Ripley Memorial Building, and her ashes were placed in the cornerstone. It is now on the National Register of Historic Places. Her wider contributions to Minnesota were recognized in 1939 when her memory was honored with a memorial plaque placed in the State Capitol.

Martha G. Ripley, M.D. Copy in Minnesota Historical Society.

Maternity Hospital Records 1885-1956, Minnesota Historical Society.

Solberg, Winton U. "Martha G. Ripley: Pioneer Doctor and Social Reformer." In *Minnesota History* 39 (Spring 1964):1-17.

Julia Bullard Nelson
(1842-1914)

by Swati Deo

*What are the obligations of the Government to me, a
widow, because my husband gave his life for it?. . . . As
a law abiding citizen and taxpayer and one who has
given all she could give to the support of this Government, I have a right to be heard. I began teaching freedmen when it was so unpopular that men would not have
done it. . . . A woman in this work gets $15 a month . . .
a man in this position receives $75 a month. There must
be something wrong, but I do not need to explain to you
that an unrepresented class must work at a disadvan-
tage. . . . If I am capable of preparing citizens, I am
capable of possessing the rights of a citizen myself.*

> - Julia Bullard Nelson in an address before a House
> of Representatives judiciary committee

Born in 1842, when the question of woman suffrage
was gaining prominence, Julia Bullard Nelson was heavily
influenced by the ideas of the movement. A woman ahead
of her time, she challenged many contemporary conventions
through logic and sheer determination in an effort to see ideas
changed about such things as equality in education. In behavior typical of her defiance against practices she considered to be wrong, Julia shortened her skirts by two inches in
order to avoid disease that could be carried in dirt. But most

of all, she sought the vote for women because she believed that legislation for other important causes would pass once women obtained the vote. As she said, "the ballot is the weapon with which to defend whatever rights we have."

Julia Bullard graduated from Hamline University, then located in Red Wing, with a teaching license. Subsequently she taught for six years in Minnesota and Connecticut before marrying Ole Nelson, a classmate and veteran of the Civil War. In 1867, a son was born to them, but tragically he did not live until his first birthday. Five months later, she was widowed at the age of twenty-six when her husband died, it is believed, of malaria contracted during the war.

Nelson returned to teaching, traveling to Texas and Tennessee to teach in freedmen's schools, eventually becoming the principal of a school in Tennessee. She strongly believed in the value of education for all, and became involved in the lives of several of her students, keeping in touch with some of them for years.

Upon her return to Minnesota in 1888, Nelson became heavily involved with the Minnesota Woman Suffrage Association (MWSA). She served as vice-president for a term, and in 1890, became the president. During her six year presidency, she petitioned every legislative session for the right to vote. Nelson also started branches of the MWSA in Blue Earth City, St. Paul and Morton. She was also the first to change the meeting places of the annual conventions, which were usually held in Minneapolis, to include cities outside the metropolitan area. In addition, for four years she edited some of the issues of the MWSA's *Minnesota Bulletin*. For a few years, she was also a lecturer for the National American Woman Suffrage Association.

In addition to her work for the MWSA, she was involved with the Woman's Christian Temperance Union (WCTU). Nelson merged the causes of temperance and suffrage, resulting in support for woman suffrage by the WCTU. She edited the *Minnesota White Ribbon*, the monthly paper of the Union, bringing the issues of suffrage to the forefront.

Nelson, through astounding determination, accomplished many goals and aided several causes over the course of her life. She often worked with individuals or groups she did not necessarily agree with in order to encourage them to look at things from a different point of view.

In her personal life, Nelson approached misfortune with courage and fortitude. After the deaths of her husband and son, she resolved to devote herself to causes that she strongly believed in. When relatives told her that it was too dangerous for a single woman to go by herself to the South following the Civil War, she insisted on going anyway. This determination continued throughout her life—despite suffering from recurring bronchitis, she agreed to go on a lecture tour in North Dakota. Unfortunately, she contracted pneumonia and died in 1914, six years before the passage of the Nineteenth Amendment.

Hurd, Ethel Edgerton. *Woman Suffrage in Minnesota: A Record of the Activities in Its Behalf Since 1847.* Minneapolis: Inland Press, 1916.

Lief, Julia W. "A Woman of Purpose: Julia B. Nelson." *Minnesota History* 47 (Winter 1981): 302-16.

Julia B. Nelson diaries in possession of her grandniece Julia W. Lief.

Gratia Countryman
(1866-1953)

by Jane Pejsa

You say that public life will destroy men's chivalry toward women. But may I ask how much chivalry is being shown to the 10,000,000 wage-earning, self-supporting women in this country who must depend upon the kindness and chivalry of men? Do you think the records of the sweated industries, the white slave traffic, show any chivalry toward woman? What would the laboring man do without the ballot to protect himself? What are these 10,000,000 laboring women doing without it? Chivalry isn't protecting them.

- From Gratia Countryman's "Liberty" talk to the all-male Intercollegiate Prohibition Association at Hamline University, 1917

Gratia Countryman was born on Thanksgiving Day, 1866. She grew up in Hastings, Minnesota, at a time of great expansion in the nation—the settling of the West as well as the early years of the industrial revolution. From childhood on Gratia held the highest expectations when it came to the human potential, not excluding her gender or herself. Her high school graduation oration carried the title "The Vocation in Which a Woman May Engage" and began:

The question is not what vocation can a woman follow by which to gain a livelihood, as if the

sphere of woman were so prescribed and narrow as to admit of little choice, but, from so
many, what one will she choose, through whose
channel she may win bread and butter and
clothes, possibly happiness and fame. . . .

Her oration continued with a list of options available to
women: teaching, especially higher education, banking, law,
medicine, writing, bookkeeping, telegraphy, and more. All
this in 1882 from a fifteen-year-old school girl.

To pinpoint the roots of the extraordinary vision exhib-
ited by this young woman from childhood on, one must look
to her father Levi Countryman. He had come from the East
to the utopian village of Nininger on the Mississippi in Minnesota. There presumably a man could work the pure soil
with his hands, at the same time elevating his mind through
study and association. But the Nininger experiment failed
and Levi was forced to find other means to support his family. Throughout Gratia's childhood and university years, he
was "on the road" across the Northwest, selling threshing
machines. Yet this father—the failed farmer turned sales-
man—clearly pointed his daughter in the direction her life
journey would take. Over a decade, in weekly letters written
from small town hotels across the West, he cajoled her, supported her, believed in her, loved her. And in a letter dated
May 22, 1885, she responded in kind:

Papa, I do so long to be more than an ordinary
woman. I do so want to fill some high position
in life. I suppose I will settle down and let my
ambitions rest unsatisfied as so many women
do though. But then a woman's position any-
where is a noble one, if she has a true concep-
tion of the meaning of life.

Gratia Countryman went on to attend the University of
Minnesota. She was such a social person as well as so socially conscious that her friends and her good works often
interfered with her studies. Countryman's extracurricular

activities included the founding of Company Q, a campus military drill unit for women, complete with uniforms and wooden guns. Her motive was to give women students the same access to physical education as their male counterparts. Male students were required to take military drill, the only physical education in the curriculum. Company Q was short-lived, however. Three years after Countryman's graduation, the Board of Regents abolished the unit, at the same time introducing physical education for women students.

Gratia Countryman graduated from the University of Minnesota in 1889 and promptly began work at the new Minneapolis Public Library, which was scheduled to open that year. She would spend forty-seven years at the library, thirty-two of them as Chief Librarian. Under her leadership the library would evolve into something quite unlike anything that had come before. The innovations that she pioneered are myriad: a state network of libraries to reach citizens in every town across Minnesota, a dedicated children's room in every library, the bookmobile, books for the street corner newsboys, books for women working in the factories and in the phone company, books in the fire stations, books in the hospitals, a reading room for the homeless, job referrals for the unemployed, foreign language materials for immigrants, and literacy training for needy adults of every stripe.

Countryman's vision for a democratic society demanded both universal suffrage and an educated electorate. Her role as Minneapolis's Chief Librarian granted her a measure of influence throughout Minnesota. Yet over the decades it was her extraordinary self-confidence combined with a winning personality that not only inspired the like-minded but also won over opponents at every level and in every place. So it had been at Hamline University in 1917:

> College men, you are open minded about almost everything; you are in the forefront in a great moral fight. Be open minded toward another great movement which is sweeping the world, democracy—this other moral move-

ment: respect the woman who studies beside you, respect the woman who may someday rear and teach your sons, respect the sanity of the campaign for freedom which womankind are making. Can you put yourselves in our place? If so, you will surely sow complete democracy. I'm for it.

The young men may have come to hear about Prohibition, but they left as converts to woman suffrage. So it would be throughout Gratia Countryman's entire life, as she chided, instructed, persuaded, and above all led in the ongoing struggle to uplift an entire citizenry and create a just society.

Benidt, Bruce Weir. *The Library Book, Centennial History of the Minneapolis Public Library*. Minneapolis: Minneapolis Public Library and Information Center, 1984.

Gratia Countryman Papers, Minnesota Historical Society.

Dyste, Mena K. "Gratia Alta Countryman, Librarian," Master's Thesis, University of Minnesota, 1965.

Pejsa, Jane. *Gratia Countryman, Her Life, Her Loves and Her Library*. Minneapolis: Nodin Press, 1995.

Rohde, Nancy Freeman. "Librarian and Reformer." In Barbara Stuhler and Gretchen Kreuter, eds., *Women of Minnesota: Selected Biographical Essays*, St. Paul: Minnesota Historical Society Press, 1977, 1998 revised.

Emily Gilman Noyes
(1854-1930)

by Rhoda Gilman

Mrs. Noyes was a very beautiful, high-minded woman. She begged me to come over to Summit Avenue where the elite lived. She wanted me to be her house guest and talk to these women about the larger views I had on suffrage and the woman question.

- Sylvie Thygeson, officer of the St. Paul Woman's Welfare League, describing Emily Gilman Noyes

Emily Hoffman Gilman came from a family that had been deeply marked by the bitterness and violence that confronted the abolition movement. Her father, as a young merchant in Alton, Illinois, had opened his warehouse to the printing press of antislavery publisher Elijah Lovejoy, and he had stood beside Lovejoy on the night the abolitionist was gunned down by a mob. Like her father, whom she idolized, Emily was ready to resist public pressure and even undertake risk on behalf of human rights. Not only was she an advocate of suffrage, but in the early twentieth century, when Minnesota law still held it a crime to share or even possess information on contraception, she joined with other prominent St. Paul women to support a clandestine birth control clinic. Their influence and social position shielded the activists who operated it and the desperate women who came there.

Born in New York City in 1854, Emily also inherited a tradition of scholarship. Her brother Arthur helped found Radcliffe College, and Benjamin, another brother, became director of the Boston Art Museum. In Emily the family talent blossomed in 1919, when she published a two-volume collection of family papers recording the role played by six generations of Gilmans in the growth of the country. Her meticulous work in selecting and editing the contents of *A Family History in Letters and Documents* was worthy of a professional historian.

In 1866 Emily's older sister Helen married Daniel Noyes of Lyme, Connecticut. Noyes was in poor health, and doctors recommended the bracing climate of Minnesota, then known for its therapeutic quality. The couple moved to St. Paul in 1868. There they were joined by Daniel's brother, Charles Noyes, and the two men formed a partnership with Edward Cutler, going into the wholesale drug business. Emily moved to Minnesota in 1874 after she married Charles.

The firm prospered, and the brothers built fine houses in the Summit Hill neighborhood and became part of the St. Paul business and cultural elite. Emily, Charles and their children traveled extensively, going frequently to Europe. Summers were often spent at White Bear Lake, where a cottage they owned is now maintained as a historic house. Affluence did not ward off sorrow, however, and their lives were shadowed by the deaths of two of their six children.

In the 1880s Emily Noyes and her sister Helen were part of a ladies' society for the discussion of literature, moral issues, and social problems. Undoubtedly one of the recurring topics was the rapid emergence of women into the urban industrial work force. Emily, however, did not stop with discussion. She played an active part in establishing the St. Paul YWCA as a residence and gathering place for young, single women.

As the struggle for suffrage gained momentum in the early years of the twentieth century, Emily Noyes became its acknowledged leader in Ramsey County. She joined with others there to found the Woman's Welfare League in 1912. At the same time she was vice president of the Minnesota Woman Suffrage Association, and in 1913-14 she became part of a small "State Central Committee" that sought to organize support for suffrage by legislative districts. In 1915, when legislative hearings on a bill for woman suffrage drew overflow crowds to the State Capitol, she was one of several state leaders who addressed the Senate committee on behalf of the measure.

Like many other suffrage advocates, however, she saw the right to vote not only as an expression of equality for women, but as a means for improving the condition of society and of families. This is evident in the announced mission of the Woman's Welfare League:

> [to] protect the interests and promote the welfare of women; to encourage the study of industrial and social conditions affecting women and the family; to enlarge the field of usefulness and activity open to women in the business and professional world; to guard them from exploitation and as a necessary means to these ends to strive to procure for women the full rights of citizenship.

Noyes served as the group's president for four years. Sylvie Thygeson, wife of a St. Paul attorney, who was vice president under Noyes, recalled later that while suffrage was the primary public thrust of the organization, its work for birth control was equally important. According to Thygeson, the organization "couldn't be identified with the birth control movement, because that was illegal, but the women who were officers all supported it."

During the final decade of her life, Noyes witnessed the triumph of the suffrage cause and was honored for her part in the long struggle. She was named honorary president of the Ramsey County Suffrage Association and of its successor, the Ramsey County League of Women Voters. Shortly before her death in 1930, she was one of six Minnesota women named to the honor roll of the National League of Women Voters.

A Family History in Letters and Documents. Copy in Minnesota Historical Society.

Gluck, Sherna, ed. *From Parlor to Prison: Five American Suffragists Talk About Their Lives.* New York: Random House, 1976.

Noyes-Gilman Ancestry. Copy in Minnesota Historical Society.

Stuhler, Barbara. *Gentle Warriors: Clara Ueland and the Minnesota Struggle for Woman Suffrage.* St. Paul: Minnesota Historical Society Press, 1995.

____. "Organizing for the Vote: Leaders of Minnesota's Woman Suffrage Movement." *Minnesota History* 54 (Fall, 1995): 299.

Ethel Edgerton Hurd
(1845-1929)

by Heidi Bauer

*We have written letters . . . licked postage stamps, trav-
eled miles and miles with petitions, given out thousands
and thousands of sheets of literature, joined in public
parades . . . we have done all this year after year, day in
and day out with no thought of self or fame . . . we have
given voluntarily and freely of our incomes, our time,
our energy, asking no return save one, the granting of
the privilege for which we struggled.*

- Ethel Edgerton Hurd, on the efforts of the Political
Equality Club of Minneapolis for woman suffrage

As one of only sixty-eight female doctors practicing in
the state of Minnesota in 1900, Ethel Edgerton Hurd was a
source of significant change in the field of medicine in the
state. Such was also true of her impact on the woman suffrage movement. A staunch opponent of the more radical
approaches of groups like the National Woman's Party, Hurd
represented the true "career" suffragist—she had been involved in the movement for decades, often working with the
same core group of women in numerous different capaci-
ties. Hurd approached her work in medicine as well as the
woman suffrage movement with a spirit of pioneering, a spirit
which developed early in her life.

Ethel Edgerton was born on August 11, 1845, in Galesburg, Illinois. In 1865 she was the first woman to graduate from Knox College in Galesburg. Shortly thereafter she married Tyrus Hurd, a railroad man, and the couple eventually settled in Minnesota. She lived a relatively quiet life until the death of her husband. Hurd then enrolled in medical school at the University of Minnesota. She continued her pioneering tradition by becoming one of the first female students to graduate from the medical school when she received her M.D. in 1897 at the age of fifty-two.

After earning her medical degree Hurd remained in Minnesota and became known as a passionate advocate for medical program reform and woman suffrage. In the medical field she led the formation of the Medical Women's Club of Minneapolis (MWCM), which presented the first public health lectures in Minnesota. The club also convinced the governor to appoint a woman to the Board of Medical Examiners. Hurd's involvement with the MWCM allowed her to develop ties to the suffrage movement, as the club was comprised of many active suffragists. The MWCM had a booth at the state fair to serve ill or injured fair-goers—it was deliberately positioned next to the booth for the Minnesota Woman Suffrage Association (MWSA).

In addition to her joint work with the MWCM and the MWSA, Hurd's early involvement in the suffrage movement was as the editor of the *Minnesota Bulletin,* a monthly newsletter from the MWSA designed to inform auxiliary clubs of executive board activities. She held this position from 1899 to 1909, when publication was discontinued due to lack of funds. She served on the Board of Directors of the MWSA as well. In addition, Hurd helped to organize the Minnesota Scandinavian Woman Suffrage Association (MSWSA) in 1907. The MSWSA recruited Scandinavian descendants, worked to influence the votes of Scandinavian politicians, and in later years raised money for the Woman Citizen's Building on the Minnesota State Fair Grounds.

Hurd continued to extend her involvement in the suffrage movement when she, along with Francis Squire Potter, helped found the Workers' Equal Suffrage Club. They had hoped to attract laborers to the group, but found that professional women such as teachers represented a majority of the members

During her suffrage career, Hurd's greatest involvement was with the Political Equality Club of Minneapolis, a group which participated in many suffragist activities such as distribution of literature, lobbying legislators and organizing parades and petition drives. As president of the Political . Equality Club of Minneapolis, Hurd helped organize events like the Historical Pageant in 1917, in which she played Elizabeth Cady Stanton. The group also sponsored a mock senate in 1914—women lawmakers argued over whether or not to grant men the right to vote. One of the major accomplishments of the club was the successful organization of the Minneapolis Woman's School and Library Organization. The purpose of this group was to nominate and support female candidates for school and library board positions, as well as register female voters to participate in these elections.

In 1916 Hurd published a book titled *Woman Suffrage in Minnesota: A Record of the Activities in Its Behalf Since 1847*, as well as a book on the history of the Political Equality Club of Minneapolis.

Through her involvement in the woman suffrage movement, Hurd had a great deal of contact with Clara Ueland. It was Hurd who wrote the first letter recommending Ueland for the presidency of the MWSA, and wrote other letters of support when Ueland faced criticism from older suffragists while in that position. She stood with Ueland when a suffrage bill came before the full Minnesota Senate in 1915; it was defeated by one vote. The two women also gave the welcome at the Mississippi Valley Suffrage Conference in 1916.

Hurd was able to see her efforts as a suffragist pay off. She was recognized as a speaker honoring suffrage pioneers at the National American Woman Suffrage Association Victory Convention just before the Nineteenth Amendment was ratified by the final states in 1920. Of the Minnesota women involved in the suffrage movement during its early stages, Hurd was the only one still alive to celebrate the passage of the Nineteenth Amendment to the U.S. Constitution.

In the midst of her political involvement, Hurd maintained her medical practice. She shared an office with her daughter Annah, who was also a doctor. Annah shared many of her mother's political beliefs and interests as well, and the two often served on the same committees.

After a long career of political activism and over thirty years in the medical field, Hurd died on August 20, 1929, while vacationing in New Brunswick, Canada. Shortly after her death, Hurd was selected as one of six Minnesotans on the honor roll for the National League of Women Voters.

Although Hurd worked tirelessly for the cause, she, along with many other suffrage leaders, did not believe that woman suffrage was the answer to all political problems. Nor did they advocate for the right to vote because they thought they could improve upon the efforts of male voters. Hurd herself said, "We anticipate many mistakes and sad blunders, but hope wisdom will come with experience." In the end, Hurd and her peers sought to win the vote simply because they believed it was their right to do so.

Hurd, Ethel Edgerton. *Woman Suffrage in Minnesota: A Record of the Activities in Its Behalf Since 1847*. Minneapolis: Inland Press, 1916.

Luth and Nanny Jaeger Papers, Minnesota Historical Society.

Stuhler, Barbara. *Gentle Warriors: Clara Ueland and the Minnesota Struggle for Woman Suffrage*. St. Paul: Minnesota Historical Society Press, 1995.

Women of Minnesota: Biographies and Sources. St. Paul: Minnesota Women's History Month, Inc., 1991.

Maud Conkey Stockwell
(1863-1958)

by Debbie Miller

After we won the right to vote, I was entertaining some friends—society people. The postman left a notice for jury duty and they began to sympathize with me, telling me I could probably get out of it. 'Get out of it?' I replied, 'I've been fighting for this opportunity for 25 years.'

> - Maud Conkey Stockwell, *Minneapolis Tribune*, May 16, 1949

When Maud Conkey Stockwell died on January 2, 1958, the day before her ninety-seventh birthday, the *Minneapolis Star* eulogized her as a "Minneapolis civic leader and supporter of woman's suffrage, disarmament, and liberal politics." Known primarily for her suffrage activity, but more radical than many in that movement, Stockwell had a lifelong interest in the causes of national suffrage leader Susan B. Anthony, and in Anthony herself. She was also active in many other organizations of establishment women, including literary clubs and the Minneapolis Beautification Club.

Perhaps the most direct connection with her history in the woman suffrage movement was the obituary's description of Stockwell as an activist in the successful 1957 campaign to name a new Minneapolis junior high school for national suffrage leader Susan B. Anthony. Earlier in her activist career, Stockwell had welcomed Anthony to a National American Woman Suffrage Association conference in Minneapolis in 1901, and when Anthony died five years later Stockwell spoke at the Minnesota memorial service. In a 1917 Political Equality Club of Minneapolis historical pageant, called "Catching Up with Father," she even played the part of Anthony.

Maud Conkey, born in Milwaukee, Wisconsin, January 3, 1863, moved with her family to Minneapolis in 1867 when her father took a job at the North Star Woolen Mill. Her parents were New Yorkers, and the family belonged to the Universalist Church. Maud was a member of the first class to graduate from the new Minneapolis Central High School. She was an enthusiastic reader and an active member of the Minneapolis Literary Club. She taught school in Minneapolis from 1882-1887, during which time she met Silvanus Stockwell and turned down his first marriage proposal. They eventually married in 1887 and the next year built a house, where they raised two daughters.

Stockwell began her political career at the turn of the century. As fellow suffragist Ethel Hurd recounted in *Woman Suffrage of Minnesota*, Stockwell served as president of the Minnesota Woman Suffrage Association (MWSA) from 1900-1910. Stockwell then served as a director and as corresponding secretary of the state executive board. She organized several suffrage clubs, including the New Era Club in Excelsior, formed in 1904, and two years later the Economic Study Club in Duluth. In 1905 she led a delegation of twenty-five women to a hearing with Governor John A. Johnson, asking him to recommend woman suffrage in his message to the legislature. Johnson failed to include the recommendation.

In addition to organizing and lobbying, Stockwell was an effective public speaker. She participated in a speaker's bureau run by the Political Equality Club of Minneapolis on the topic "Suffrage in Practice." In 1910, says Hurd, "Mrs.

Stockwell addressed the Northern Minnesota Reapportionment and Development Congress at Bemidji on 'Sex Reapportionment.' At the close of her address 50 men signed the petition to Congress for woman suffrage." In another sketch of Stockwell's work for suffrage, Hurd noted that "Mrs. Stockwell took the great roll [of 20,500 Minnesota signatures] to Washington, D.C. and rode in the mile long procession of automobiles that carried the delegates with their rolls of petitions to the capitol," where a congressman from each state presented them to the Congress.

As president of the MWSA, wrote her grandson William Everts many years later, "Maud Stockwell spoke out on a wide range of equal rights issues." For example, she used her considerable moral authority to stand up for Gratia Countryman in 1903, when Countryman was appointed the first woman to be chief librarian of the Minneapolis Public Library, but allotted only two-thirds the salary of her male predecessor and deprived of an assistant. Stockwell came to the defense of this victim of turn-of-the-century sexism, as reported in the *Minneapolis Journal*:

> I am much gratified to learn that the library board has recognized Miss Countryman's real worth and the valuable service she has rendered to the library by appointing her librarian. The action in cutting her salary and giving the new librarian the work of two persons shows a most unjust discrimination against women and every high-minded citizen should protest against such injustice.

Stockwell's husband Silvanus was an early supporter of woman suffrage, introducing a bill into the Minnesota legislature in 1891 to confer municipal suffrage on women, which went nowhere, as well as a successful bill in 1902 to give women co-guardianship of minor children. Ethel Hurd assessed her colleague's work with the MWSA: "The ten years of Mrs. Stockwell's presidency were characterized by persistent, quiet, earnest endeavor. The utmost harmony prevailed, and the rapid advance of the cause today, its popularity and promise of success bear testimony to the efficiency of her labor."

After the ratification of the Nineteenth Amendment, Maud Stockwell went right on working for liberal and even radical causes. In 1922 she was a founder and served as first chair of the Minnesota section of the Women's International League for Peace and Freedom. She was a member of the National Child Labor Committee and served on the board of the Minnesota Birth Control League, a forerunner of Planned Parenthood. Her long memory and years of activism served Stockwell and her community well. An accepted member of Minneapolis's establishment, Stockwell used her elite status to work for a variety of causes, with woman suffrage being the first.

Everts, William P. Jr., *Stockwell of Minneapolis: A Pioneer of Social and Political Consciousness*. St. Cloud, Minn.: North Star Press, 1996.

Hurd, Ethel Edgerton. *Woman Suffrage in Minnesota: A Record of the Activities in Its Behalf Since 1847*. Minneapolis: Inland Press, 1916.

Obituary, *Minneapolis Star*, 3 January 1958.

Obituary, *Minneapolis Morning Tribune*, 3 January 1958.

Minnesota Woman Suffrage Association Records (microfilm edition), Minnesota Historical Society.

Pejsa, Jane. *Gratia Countryman: Her Life, Her Loves and Her Library*. Minneapolis: Nodin Press, 1995.

Political Equality Club of Minneapolis Records, Minnesota Historical Society.

Stuhler, Barbara and Gretchen Kreuter, eds. *Women of Minnesota: Selected Biographical Essays*. St. Paul: Minnesota Historical Society Press, 1977, 1998 revised.

Maria Sanford
(1836-1920)

by *Arvonne Fraser*

Work is life to me. It always has been and always will be.

- Maria Sanford in a 1916 public press response to letters on her eightieth birthday

Maria Sanford came late to the suffrage movement, not announcing her support until 1912 during a speech at the General Federation of Women's Clubs conference in San Francisco—she was seventy-six years old. Although she enjoyed and even cultivated public attention, Sanford was more determined about women accepting responsibilities as respectable public citizens than in achieving their rights. A woman of contradictions, she became a beloved symbol and role model of the modern American woman with strong support from women's clubs and students.

In 1942, a generation after her death, the Minnesota Federation of Women's Clubs passed a resolution urging that a statue of Maria Sanford be placed in National Statuary Hall in the U.S. Capitol. The resolution was honored in 1958, Minnesota's centennial year, when Sanford was chosen as one of the two statues representing Minnesota. At the time, she was only the second woman in the nation so honored.

Her statue's inscription identifies her as:

> [A] sturdy and resilient Puritan, whose perceptive mind and reverence for classic truth and beauty quickened intellectual life within the pioneer state of Minnesota and beyond its frontiers. Educator, orator, civic leader, the best-known and best-loved woman in Minnesota.

One can guess that Maria Sanford would have been extremely pleased with that description of herself. While publicly stating that a woman's "highest duty [is] to make [the] home happy for husband and children" she lived a very different life. Born on December 18, 1836, in Connecticut, Maria was educated in country schools. She graduated with honors from the New Britain Normal School in 1855 and began teaching for a salary of ten dollars a month. Gradually she worked her way up the professional ladder.

A charismatic but demanding teacher admired by students, parents and school officials, she was recruited in 1869 to run as elected school superintendent in a Pennsylvania county, a rare event for a woman. Although she campaigned vigorously, visiting every voter, she lost by a narrow margin. Later that same year she was appointed to teach English and history at Swarthmore College, and the next year was offered the position of professor of history, becoming one of the country's first female college professors.

Sanford also began lecturing outside the classroom, first to teachers' groups and then to the general public. At this time public speaking by women was considered almost immoral, but what she had to say was conventional wisdom. She rocked no boats, but she was a brilliant orator, a tiny woman who always dressed in simple, long black dresses and could project her voice to the farthest corners of any large hall. A believer in lifelong learning, she considered her public speaking an extension of her teaching, which occasionally gave her difficulties with college administrators who thought she was neglecting her teaching duties and earning too much on the lecture circuit. At both Swarthmore and later the University of Minnesota she had her teaching salary, but not her teaching load, reduced because she spent so much time on the paid lecture circuit.

In 1880, Sanford was recruited by the president of the University of Minnesota as one of its first female professors, even though she had no college degree. Later she was appointed head of the University's English department where she taught composition, rhetoric, elocution, and oratory. Her tenure at the University was not without contention, however. She fought the regents over her pay and pension, believing in women's right to equal pay, sometimes charged her students fees for extra tutoring, and ran a rooming house for students where she allowed dancing. But she endeared herself to the majority of her students with her wide-ranging scholarship, and her challenging and innovative teaching methods, including the very early use of lantern slides to illustrate her lectures on art and architecture. She endeared herself with the public with her lecturing and her promotion of community improvement and American cultural values.

A passionate advocate of public education and member of countless women's clubs, she knew how to use the media to promote women's causes as well as herself. A consummate politician—though not by her own definition—she was also a woman who promoted civil rights before that term was ever invented, raising money for Southern black churches and American Indian child health care. Although Sanford earned a salary and lectured for money, she spent most of her life in debt as a result of a series of unwise real estate investments. She also assisted relatives and students financially, and was admired for refusing to file bankruptcy. Sanford preached and practiced responsibility, believing that responsibilities took precedence over rights.

Upon retiring from the University of Minnesota at age seventy-three, university officials were forced to put aside their frustration with her unconventional teaching methods because of her popularity, and Sanford was made professor emeritus of rhetoric in 1909. Her next career was lecturing full time to make enough money to pay her debts. Although she traveled all over the country, she prefered the West, believing that it was the land of opportunity for women, given that many western states had granted women the right to vote. After seeing what these voting women had done for their communities, Sanford spoke out for woman's suffrage in San Francisco. She continued lecturing across the country promoting education, child welfare, woman's suffrage and public responsibility. In her late seventies she ventured to Montana at considerable inconvenience to herself to lecture in rural areas. Still, she considered Minneapolis her home and spent countless hours during her retirement giving individual attention to students of the Maria Sanford Elementary School in North Minneapolis.

After her retirement, her birthdays were often celebrated in Minneapolis as public events. On her eightieth birthday the University held a convocation celebrating her career. A semi-humorous poem read at that event described her thundering voice, called her "vehement and gusty, leonine, hale and lusty," a woman with a drove of causes who kept a tally of reforms but could unleash a "hurricane of laughter."

Maria Sanford died quietly in her sleep in 1920 in a Washington, D.C. hotel room the night after giving a speech to the Daughters of the American Revolution national convention. Although she didn't live to become a voter, she was known to public officials and citizens alike as a woman of influence.

Hartley, Lucie. *Maria Sanford: Pioneer Professor*. Minneapolis: Dillon Press, 1977.

Maria Sanford Papers, Minnesota Historical Society.

Shapiro, Maude Shirley. "A Rhetorical Critical Analysis of the Lecturing of Maria Louise Sanford." Ph.D. diss., University of Minnesota, 1959.

Schofield, Geraldine Bryan and Susan Margot Smith. "Maria Louise Sanford: Minnesota's Heroine." In Barbara Stuhler and Gretchen Kreuter, eds., *Women of Minnesota: Selected Biographical Essays*. St. Paul: Minnesota Historical Society Press, 1977, 1998 revised.

Whitney, Helen. *Maria Sanford*. Minneapolis: University of Minnesota Press, 1922.

Winning the
Vote

Nanny Mattson Jaeger
(1859-1938)

by Marjorie Bingham

A little suffrage spice into the melting pot . . .

- Nanny Mattson Jaeger's description of the Minnesota Scandinavian Woman Suffrage Association

Nanny Mattson Jaeger was particularly noted for her presidency of the Minnesota Scandinavian Woman Suffrage Association (MSWSA). While this organization was closely linked to the Minnesota Woman Suffrage Association, Jaeger and others felt it was important to have a separate organization to appeal to voters of Scandinavian background.

Indeed, Scandinavian legislators were likely to support woman suffrage partly because by 1913 Finland and Norway had already approved the enfranchisement of women, and Sweden and Denmark seemed likely to follow. Jaeger believed that these international connections between "the old countries and ourselves" would make for an "international solidarity of women." Jaeger acted as a link between these countries by soliciting and then circulating a message from Ellen Key, the noted Swedish suffragist, supporting Minnesota women's efforts. Earlier, as president of the Political Equality Club of Minneapolis, Jaeger had also shown international concern by supporting the English suffragists imprisoned and force-fed while serving their sentence under a hunger strike. It was, she denounced, "barbarous treatment from their government."

Perhaps Jaeger's interest in international issues had been fostered by her early education in Sweden. Though born in Red Wing, Nanny went to school in Sweden between 1871-76. Back in Minnesota, she became the first women of Scandinavian background to enter the University of Minnesota when she enrolled in 1877. She later wrote that her parents contributed to her own interests. Her father was connected to Swedish newspapers and her mother was a strong feminist. Jaeger said, "It was largely due to early training in this respect that I became an ardent suffrage worker." Nanny married Luth Jaeger while at the University, and their children engaged most of her attention early in their marriage. Luth was a strong supporter of woman suffrage and his views on the issue were frequently used by Minnesota suffragist organizers in swaying Swedish churches and Scandinavian male audiences.

Nanny Jaeger came to make suffrage her main organizational focus, considering the issue "the most important and constructive of my generation." She led the MSWSA in its drive to fund a Woman Citizen Building at the Minnesota State Fair Grounds. The purpose of the building was to have "a suitable and dignified" place for suffrage workers and women to use for longer conversations and rest. At the dedication of the building, Jaeger used the occasion to remind the audience that Scandinavian immigrant women applying for citizenship were still asked, "Which man do you belong to?" The suggestion was that they would only become citizens through their husband's actions and not their own. As Jaeger put it, "But how about the women? Are they less loyal? Have they equal opportunities with their brother?"

Though the creation of the Woman Citizen Building was a success, Jaeger's presidency was not without controversy. The complete funding of the building had put a strain on

MSWSA finances, but more controversial was the split over Alice Paul and the picketing of the White House by the National Woman's Party during World War I. Jaeger supported the picketers, believing they made the suffrage issue more visible, but there were some who resigned from the organization, seeing the protests as unpatriotic in wartime. In spite of the problems she encountered, Jaeger saw the MSWSA through to the passage of the Nineteenth Amendment. She continued to develop and utilize ties to the Scandinavian community and often had members of the MSWSA dress in Scandinavian costumes for suffrage parades.

Later, Brenda Ueland, daughter of Jaeger's suffragist friend Clara Ueland, reflected on the qualities Jaeger brought to the suffrage movement. Jaeger, she thought, was "rather formidable," "piercingly and ironically intelligent—she had a volatile, immediate laugh that made others feel witty." Jaeger brought all these talents and her Scandinavian heritage to the woman suffrage movement. Her later activities included being a director of the Women's Christian Association. Jaeger died in Minneapolis, May 16, 1938.

Foster, Mary Dillon, ed. *Who's Who Among Minnesota Women.* N.p.: Privately Published, 1924.

Hurd, Ethel Edgerton. *Woman Suffrage in Minnesota: A Record of the Activities in Its Behalf Since 1847.* Minneapolis: Inland Press, 1916.

Luth and Nanny Jaeger Papers, Minnesota Historical Society.

Minneapolis Tribune, 17 May 1938.

Ueland, Brenda. "Clara Ueland of Minnesota." 1967. Copy in Minnesota Historical Society.

Josephine Sarles Simpson
(1862-1948)

by Norma Sommerdorf

*May it not be that the time has come for the methods
and ideals of the family to become the methods and ideals of the nation? Nature commands and our hearts re-
spond to the call of women to the care of the home and
the education of children. But is it not possible that they
shall push the walls of that home farther and farther
out, until it shall include the whole nation, even all the
nations of the world?*

- Josephine Sarles Simpson

Josephine Sarles Simpson became one of the chief ora-
tors for the suffrage movement in Minnesota and other states.
Then, during the years Carrie Chapman Catt was heading
the National American Woman Suffrage Association
(NAWSA), Josephine Sarles Simpson traveled as a lecturer
in New York and other areas.

Josephine Sarles was born in Necedah, Wisconsin, in
1862. She would later say that when she was ten years old
she asked her father why women were not allowed to vote,
to which he replied, "My child, there are no reasons why
women shouldn't vote." She received a Bachelor of Laws
degree from the University of Wisconsin with highest honors, then moved to Minnesota in 1884. She was married to

David Simpson on January 14, 1886, and they had three sons.

Simpson became active in the Mother's Council when her children were young, inspecting sanitation of public school buildings. Her first report created a demand for a woman on the school board, and she was one of the founders of the Minneapolis Free Kindergarten Association. As a member of the Minneapolis Improvement League she was responsible for the distribution of flower seeds to 10,000 Minneapolis children.

A very active woman, Simpson was a charter member of the Woman's Club of Minneapolis. From 1907-08 she served as the director of the Social Economics Department of the Club, and from 1908-10 she served as chair of that same department. In 1908 the Social Economics Department formed a committee on "Pure Water Supply for Minneapolis," which led to the formation of a Pure Water Commission, on which Simpson served. The next year the State Labor Bureau requested the help of the Social Economics Department in researching the conditions of child workers. Simpson also chaired committees on the regulation of billboards, antismoking action, and health surveys.

Due to her political activism, Simpson was considered as a presidential candidate for the Woman's Club of Minneapolis by the nominating committee. However, despite their notable work regarding social issues, the Woman's Club of Minneapolis was not a suffrage society, and there were some members who were against woman suffrage. The nominating committee decided not to nominate Simpson because she took "such a strong stand on the woman suffrage question," and they were afraid of offending members who didn't share her views.

An active member of the Republican Woman's Club, Simpson was appointed by Governor Adolph O. Eberhart to be a delegate to the First Minnesota Conservation and Agricultural Development Congress, and by Governor Jacob A. A. Preus to the State Crime Commission. She was a member of the Women's Trade Union League, which provided funds for women workers in industry to attend summer sessions at Bryn Mawr College in Pennsylvania.

While attending the University of Wisconsin, Simpson was awarded the Burrows Prize for oratory in 1883. This gift for oration won her admiration, and helped her advance the cause of suffrage. A newspaper article once described her as "a lady of commanding presence, an easy, graceful, impressive speaker, who frequently and without effort rises to heights of oratory." Between 1915-17 she used this talent as a lecturer in New York during the important referendum campaigns. During this time she also traveled by steamboat down the Mississippi with a contingent of Minnesota suffragists to speak outside the Democratic convention in St. Louis, Missouri, which convened on June 14, 1916. Simpson and others spoke to the crowd of delegates from their cars and from a makeshift bandstand in front of hotel headquarters.

Between 1918 and 1920, as victory was beginning to look imminent, Simpson served on the board of directors of the NAWSA. On September 8, 1919, when the state of Minnesota ratified the Nineteenth Amendment, Simpson told the press: "I feel today as one who has come into a great inheritance after being a political pauper; I have such a feeling of comfort and power and dignity." Simpson concluded her suffrage career as president of the Hennepin County Woman Suffrage Association.

Simpson's husband David was the Minneapolis City Attorney and later a member of the Minnesota Supreme Court. He died as the result of an automobile accident in 1925. After her husband's death, Simpson moved to Pasadena, California and for the next twenty years continued to speak out on women's issues. She also served as president of the Wisconsin Alumni in California. She died in Pasadena in 1948.

Foster, Mary Dillon, ed. *Who's Who Among Minnesota Women.* N.p.: Privately Published, 1924.

Ludcke, Jeannette. *You've Come a Long Way, Lady!: The Seventy-Five Year History of the Woman's Club of Minneapolis.* Minneapolis: The Club, 1982.

David Ferguson Simpson Papers, Minnesota Historical Society.

Stuhler, Barbara. *Gentle Warriors: Clara Ueland and the Minnesota Struggle for Woman Suffrage.* St. Paul: Minnesota Historical Society Press, 1995.

Fanny Fligelman Brin
(1884-1961)

---

by Barbara Stuhler

When I was quite young, I heard notes which say to women to seek their full development in the educational, the professional, the political field.

- Fanny Fligelman Brin

Fanny Fligelman Brin was one of three remarkable women of Minneapolis who emerged from the suffrage movement to take leadership roles on the national scene as presidents of influential women's organizations: the General Federation of Women's Clubs headed by Alice Ames Winter (1920-24); the National League of Women Voters led by Marguerite Milton Wells (1934-44); and the National Council of Jewish Women chaired by Fanny Fligelman Brin (1932-38). The presidency of the Council proved to be a midpoint in Fanny Brin's lifelong journey of service to the four drummers to whose beat she marched: women's rights, Judaism, democracy, and world peace.

Fanny Fligelman arrived in the United States from Romania in 1884 at the early age of three months. Her father urged her to talk "United States" and helped shape her oratorical and debating skills by his own delight in serious debate and discussion. Her mother encouraged her to "play school" and be the teacher. By this ruse, Fanny later realized, her mother learned to speak and read English.

Given her family's intellectual interests and the priority they gave to education, it is not surprising that Fanny attended the University of Minnesota. It was there—influenced by prominent suffragists on the faculty like professors Maria Sanford and Frances Squire Potter—that Fanny became active in the movement to win votes for women. She proved to be bright, winning a Phi Beta Kappa key in her senior year, and displayed a gift for oratory, becoming the first woman to succeed in the University's famed Pillsbury oratorical contest where she won the second prize of $50 for her presentation on "Russian Bureaucracy and the Jews." Her speaking skills were one of the attributes of leadership that won acolytes to the various causes she championed throughout her life. A year after her graduation in 1907, she received a teaching certificate and taught first in Northfield and then at West High School in Minneapolis.

As a young career woman, Fanny Fligelman was active but not prominent in the suffrage movement. In 1909 she gave a speech at the convention of the Minnesota Woman Suffrage Association titled "Is Woman the Ward or Companion of Man?" Given her commitment to equal rights, one can assume she answered "companion." Subsequently, Fanny served as a member of the board of directors of the state association. In 1912, she became president of the Workers' Equal Suffrage Club, a small organization intending to attract working women of all classes to the suffrage cause.

Fanny once commented, "it was good to follow . . . such fine women as Mrs. [Maud] Stockwell, Mrs. Andreas [Clara] Ueland, and Mrs. Frances Squire Potter." These women heightened Fanny's sense of what women could achieve. She noticed that although "we seem to be moving very slowly, I have faith that women will someday make a great contribution to civilization. The need for women's participation grows daily. . . . I believe they can do more than they realize."

When Fanny Fligelman married Arthur Brin in 1913, there was a hiatus in her activity following the births of one daughter and two sons. By the time she renewed her role as a volunteer in community affairs, votes for women had been won, and she turned her attention to the Minneapolis Council of Jewish Women, the first step in her election some years later as president of the national organization. It was a fitting place for Brin to continue her concerns for women who still suffered a number of disadvantages in the struggle to achieve equality.

Brin understood that women's long dependence had given them a sense of inferiority, but she was confident that education would dispel that lack of self-esteem. She laughed scornfully at the suggestion that the newly invented baby carriage would destroy the whole fabric of family life by permitting a mother to go outside the home. Nor did she believe that domesticity was necessarily woman's destiny and asked, "How can we be in the world and not of it?" Neither did she view the feminist movement as a disparagement of man. Instead, she felt that with women assuming a larger place in society, they should be concerned with building and changing society "so that men and women will have a world in which they can live happily, creatively, securely." As long ago as 1933 she foresaw a future movement arising out of the need for orderly planing of "a new social order in which men and women shall share alike."

Her leadership of the National Council of Jewish Women was shared with her concern in the late 1930s and 1940s for the plight of the Jewish refugees. In 1923, she had been inspired by a speech of Carrie Chairman Catt urging the National Council and its members to turn their efforts to world peace. Brin made that commitment, and in the years between the two great wars as well as after World War II, by the example of her persistence and the eloquence of her persuasion, she rallied many American women to work on behalf of international arrangements to resolve conflict and prevent the outbreak of future wars.

Fanny Brin's list of appointments, organizational offices, and honors reflect the depth of her commitment and her influence both in Minnesota and on the national scene. She was a mid-century Jewish activist, a personification of the citizen-advocate, a feminist, and an exemplary leader.

Brin, Fanny. Speech, November, 1937. Fanny Brin Papers, Minnesota Historical Society.

Hurd, Ethel Edgerton. *Woman Suffrage in Minnesota: A Record of the Activities in Its Behalf Since 1847.* Minneapolis: Inland Press, 1916.

Smith, K.M. "Tsedakah: Lives of Social Justice," in *Hennepin History* 50, no. 5 (Winter 1992).

Stuhler, Barbara. "Fanny Brin: Woman of Peace." In Barbara Stuhler and Gretchen Kreuter, eds., *Women of Minnesota: Selected Biographical Essays.* St. Paul: Minnesota Historical Society Press, 1977, 1998 revised.

Josephine Schain
(1886-1972)

---

by Norma Sommerdorf and Sheila Ahlbrand

When we ask for the ballot we are not advocating an easy life for women. Great characters are developed through responsibility. The ballot is a responsibility. Greater womanhood will be more fully developed through a better understanding of the world's problems. The age of cloistered innocence has passed. The need is for women, as well as men, who will help in the solution of the world's work.

- Josephine Schain, in a debate on "The Advantages of Equal Suffrage," at the University of Minnesota, 1914

An active suffragist in the state of Minnesota, Josephine Schain moved to New York in 1915 as a close associate of Carrie Chapman Catt. Catt had just begun her second term as president of the National American Woman Suffrage Association (NAWSA). Although there was a spread of twenty-seven years in their ages, they worked together in the woman's suffrage movement, training women for direct social action until the Nineteenth Amendment was adopted in 1920.

Josephine Schain was born in Brown's Valley, Minnesota in 1886. She graduated from the University of Minnesota in 1907, and received an M.A. in International Law in

1908. Upon graduation her first position was as head of the Municipal Research Department of the Minneapolis Public Library.

Schain's interests often brought her into the realm of social service. She was a legal aid for the Associated Charities of Minneapolis, and served on the executive board of the Hennepin County Juvenile Protection Association. For two years she lived and worked at the Pillsbury House, a settlement house in Minneapolis, in order to "really know the people" who lived there. Her knowledge of the law and her interest in social service came together in a volume she prepared called *Laws of Minnesota Relating to Women and Children*.

Schain saw the fight for woman suffrage as an extension of her social work. She believed that women could use "the ballot as a tool for bringing about social betterment." From 1909 to 1912 Schain served as the secretary to the Minnesota Woman Suffrage Association (MWSA), and in 1913 was elected as chair of the education committee. Although after 1913 Schain no longer served on the executive board of the MWSA, she remained very active within the organization.

One of the big events in Minnesota in 1914 was a suffrage parade through the streets of Minneapolis on May 2. As general marshall of the parade Schain led nearly 2,000 people on a route from Second Avenue to Fourth Street, and back on Nicollet Avenue to the city auditorium. Later, in December of 1914, Schain, along with Clara Ueland, participated in an important debate on the issue of woman's suffrage held at the University of Minnesota, where they argued their case opposite Lavinia Coppock Gilfillan and Florence Welles Carpenter, two of the leading advocates of the anti-suffrage movement.

The following year a state chapter of the Congressional Union, the national organization founded by radical suffragist Alice Paul, was formed in Minnesota, with Schain counted among its members. The Congressional Union held the party in office accountable for not passing woman suffrage, and campaigned against them in an effort to bring about change. As a member of the Congressional Union, Schain organized processions to the offices of local representatives, as well as large street meetings in such outlying communities as Le Sueur and Shakopee.

By the end of 1915, at the age of twenty-nine, Schain had moved to New York City to work for the cause of woman suffrage on the national level. It was there that she met her mentor, Carrie Chapman Catt, a native of Wisconsin, educated at Iowa State College, and president of the NAWSA. Ironically, Catt believed that the suffragists should support the party in power, the opposite strategy of the Congressional Union. Therefore, when Schain moved to New York City, she changed not only her place of residence, but her suffrage strategies as well.

But some things never change. While in New York City, Schain lived for a time at the Henry Street Settlement, continuing her social work, while the activities of the rest of her life revealed her continued interest in politics and women's issues. When the National League of Women Voters was formed following the passage of the Nineteenth Amendment Schain became Director of International Cooperation.

Catt continued to be a major influence in her life, and Schain worked with her closely on the National Committee on the Causes and Cure of War (NCCCW), an organization founded by Catt in 1925. In 1926 Schain attended sessions of the League of Nations and the International Institute at Geneva, and traveled through Central Europe, the Balkans, and the Middle East.

Josephine Schain was selected to become national director of the Girl Scouts in 1933, a position she held until 1935, when she resigned in order to become chair of the NCCCW. That same year she served as chair of the U.S. Delegation to the Conference of the International Alliance of Women. In 1943 as the U.S. Delegate to the World Conference of Food and Agriculture, she became the first woman to officially represent the United States at any United Nations Conference, and in 1945 was a Consultant at the formation of the United Nations. She was president of the Pan Pacific Women's Association from 1949 to 1953, and a member of the Democratic National Committee from 1940 to 1946.

Josephine Schain continued working until 1971, only a year before her death. Her many accomplishments in social work, the peace movement, international affairs, and her work with girls are proof that she took her own words seriously, becoming a woman who indeed helped "in the solution of the world's work."

Clippings from the files of the Girl Scouts USA.

"High Power Woman Power," *Independent Woman*, July 1943.

Minnesota Alumni Weekly 21 (November 1936): 197.

Schain, Josephine. "The Advantages of Equal Suffrage." In J.F. Ebersole, ed., *Papers and Proceedings of the Eighth Annual Meeting of the Minnesota Academy of Social Sciences*. General Topic: "Women and the State." Publications of the Minnesota Academy of Social Sciences, vol. 8, no. 8. Mankato, Minn.: Published for the Academy by the Free Press Printing Co., 1915.

_____. "Vocations Open to Women," Bulletin of the University of Minnesota, extra series no. 1.

Josephine Schain Papers, Sophia Smith Collection, Smith College.

Van Voris, Jacqueline. *Carrie Chapman Catt: A Public Life*. New York: The Feminist Press at The City University of New York, 1987.

Sarah Tarleton Colvin

(1865-1949)

by Mary Pruitt

*President Wilson is deceiving the world. He preaches
democracy abroad and thwarts democracy at home.*

-Sarah Tarleton Colvin's banner while picketing
at the White House, February 9, 1919

At age fifty-one, Sarah Colvin chafed at what she called
"the wastefulness of women's lives." Her response was to
direct her anger into movements for social justice. Her energies as an activist were applied towards medical issues and
the woman's suffrage movement.

Born in Green County, Alabama, in 1865, Sarah Tarleton
had a memorable childhood. Her father, retired from the
Confederate Army and managing a plantation, died when
she was only three, leaving her mother with three young
children to raise. In 1887 Sarah traveled across Europe for
two years with her mother and sister. Rebelling against the
conservative views of her family, who believed that women
should demonstrate "feminine qualities of submission," Sarah chose to enroll in the first nurses training class at Johns
Hopkins University in 1890. After graduation, Sarah served
as a private nurse, working at hospitals in New York City
and Montreal, Canada. She met her future husband in Canada.

Dr. Alexander Colvin and Sarah Tarleton were married in 1897 and moved to St. Paul, Minnesota, that same year.

In Minnesota, Sarah Colvin's activism began with medical issues. She helped form the Minnesota Graduate Nursing Association, which eventually became the Minnesota Nurses Association. Colvin also supported Margaret Sanger's new birth control clinics, developed a visiting nurse service and founded Lake Owassa Tuberculosis Clinic.

Colvin also became involved in the woman suffrage movement, and the Minnesota Congressional Union invited her to be their president in 1916. The national office of the Congressional Union appointed her Chair of the North Middle Western States District. Compared to other suffrage groups of the time, the Congressional Union took a more radical approach, which suited Colvin's political skills.

Through the Congressional Union, Colvin created suffrage enthusiasm at meetings in Wisconsin, Iowa, Illinois, Missouri, Louisiana, Alabama, and South Carolina. In Minnesota Colvin staged luncheons and rallies attracting hundreds of women and men. She opened a new headquarters in St. Paul to symbolize the distance from the Minnesota Woman Suffrage Association (MWSA), the moderate mainstream suffrage group based in Minneapolis. Over the door of the new headquarters Colvin flew a banner announcing the Congressional Union's commitment to their federal strategy: "We demand an amendment to the United States Constitution enfranchising women."

In 1917 the Congressional Union merged with the Woman's Party; the new group was called the National Woman's Party (NWP). The Minnesota branch became the Minnesota Woman's Party (MWP). President Wilson finally extended his support to the federal suffrage amendment in 1918, and Congress voted on the issue. The House of Representatives passed the amendment, but it was defeated by the Senate. Colvin, along with Bertha Moller of the MWP, Rhoda Kellogg, president of the Equal Suffrage Association at the University of Minnesota, and Gertrude Murphy, Superintendent of Music in the Minneapolis schools, traveled from Minnesota to Washington, D.C. to picket; they were arrested and spent time in jail. Twenty-five activists from across the state of Minnesota raised thousands of dollars to support the picketers. Newspapers labeled them traitors. Clara Ueland called them the "lunatic fringe." The MWP felt that such drastic action was the only way they could be effective.

The national marches continued, and in late January, 1919, Colvin was arrested for burning President Wilson in effigy and sentenced to five days in jail. Her actions were part of what the NWP called the "Watchfire for Freedom." The demonstration was lined up on the sidewalk in front of the White House along the sight line to the President's front door for dramatic visual effect. Colvin's jail sentence was "indescribably revolting." She said, "I believe I have the distinction of being the only suffragist who was ever alone in jail." Worms swam in the food. Colvin, as was typical of many jailed suffragists, went on a hunger strike. The jail "was full of rats and I minded them more than anything else," she said.

In spite of her trying experience, Colvin risked jail again in February by participating in what she called "the largest and most spectacular demonstration we pulled off." Colvin wired her Minnesota colleague Emily Bright: "I am just out of jail . . . twenty-six sentenced. Feel the trip very important now."

After another five days in jail, Colvin reveled in one more bold suffrage campaign. The NWP created a "Prison Special" train to show off the courage of the political prisoners. The MWP raised $300 of the $20,000 budget. Colvin delivered suffrage speeches from the observation platform of the train they called "Democracy Limited." Sarah Colvin proudly wore her costume: a replica of her prison uniform.

As president of the MWP, Sarah Colvin presided over an organization that represented a modest 800 Minnesota members compared to the 15,000 of the MWSA. The tactics of the MWP and MWSA may have differed greatly, but the combined efforts of the two groups provided dramatic results. The MWP had a much smaller roster, but its members are credited with being more focused, as well as winning over former political enemies.

Colvin's political action extended into other areas once woman suffrage was obtained. She was a member of the Minnesota State Board of Education from 1935-41. She resigned in protest over what she believed was political control over of the board. She wrote of her political activities in her autobiography, *A Rebel in Thought*, published in 1944. Colvin died in St. Paul in 1949.

Colvin, Sarah Tarleton. *A Rebel in Thought*. New York: Island Press, 1944.

Irwin, Inez Haynes. *The Story of Alice Paul and the National Women's* [sic] *Party*. Fairfax, Va.: Denlinger's Publishers, LTD, 1977.

Minnesota Woman Suffrage Association Records (microfilm edition), Minnesota Historical Society.

National Woman's Party Papers, Library of Congress.

Minnesota Commission of Public Safety Papers, Minnesota Historical Society.

Stevens, Doris. *Jailed For Freedom*. New York: Boni and Lieright Publishers, 1920.

Stuhler, Barbara. *Gentle Warriors: Clara Ueland and the Minnesota Struggle for Woman Suffrage*. St. Paul: Minnesota Historical Society Press, 1995.

The Suffragist, 15 February 1916.

"Congressional Union Officers," *The Suffragist*, 1 April 1916.

"Prohibition Party Adopts Iron-Clad Suffrage Plank," *The Suffragist*, 29 July 1916.

"The Prison Special," *The Suffragist*, 15 February 1919.

Clara Hampson Ueland
(1860-1927)

❦

by Barbara Stuhler

I would like to do a little something for the cause.

- Clara Hampson Ueland on her work for woman's
suffrage

Clara Ueland made her mark as an activist concerned
with community betterment. She worked on behalf of kindergartens, the preservation of immigrant crafts and support
for the fine arts, clean air and clean water, prison reform,
community charities, the abolishment of billboards, the formation of a juvenile court, and more efficient and effective
municipal government. And all the while she was also taking care of a large household populated by her affable husband and seven talented children. Her greatest achievement
in the public realm proved to be her leadership of the woman
suffrage movement in Minnesota. She led the effort in its
final years and could taste the sweet fruit of victory when
votes for women became the law of the land in 1920.

With her widowed mother and older brother, Clara
Hampson came to Minnesota from Ohio, settling first in
Faribault and then in Minneapolis, where they lived in a small
apartment over a hardware store in a disreputable area of the
city. Maud Conkey Stockwell, a suffragist who had been a

school friend, remembered "thinking how incongruous she was with all the saloons around that district. She was dark and slim, a beauty beyond compare." Despite her surroundings and continuing poverty, Clara was happy in school and was a well-adjusted young woman. It tells something about Clara's character that she refused other invitations to a junior class dance to go with the only African American boy in the school because she felt he needed friendship and support.

Lacking the resources to continue her education, Clara turned to teaching as a career and, eight years later in 1885, married Andreas Ueland, a Norwegian immigrant, who had studied law at night while working during the day as a common laborer. In the sixteen years between 1886 and 1902, eight children were born, one of whom died in early childhood. Although Ueland's civic activism was slowed by the responsibilities of a growing family, she put her experience as an educator and her ideals as a thoughtful and well-read woman to work at home. She saw the need for early childhood education, establishing a neighborhood kindergarten and providing leadership for the effort that resulted in the integration of kindergartens in the Minneapolis public schools in 1895.

Although she became increasingly engaged in community affairs she was not an early suffragist. Aware of the movement, she did not get caught up in it until her college-age daughters began to express their interest (one daughter, Elsa, was president of the University of Minnesota's Equal Suffrage Association). Ueland's initiative in forming the Equal Suffrage Association of Minneapolis in 1913 was followed by her agreement the following year to serve as the thirteenth and last president of the Minnesota Woman Suffrage Association (MWSA).

Ueland's commitment as leader of the Minnesota movement made a difference. She was a respectful listener and a persuasive advocate. Both the 1915 and 1917 legislative sessions had been suffrage cliffhangers. In 1915, suffrage was defeated in the Senate by one vote and won in the House by a majority, but not by the necessary two-thirds required for passage. In 1917, the House passed one suffrage measure but the Senate failed by four votes to pass the presidential suffrage bill supported by the MWSA. Undaunted, Ueland's political acumen, determination, organizational skills, and her ability to inspire women to even greater efforts finally set the stage for victory. In 1919, the legislature overwhelmingly adopted a joint resolution urging Congress to submit a federal suffrage amendment to the states for ratification, and then passed legislation, approving woman suffrage in presidential elections (the House vote was 103 to 24, the Senate vote 49 to 11).

On September 8, Governor Joseph A. A. Burnquist called the legislature into special session where it ratified the Nineteenth Amendment—in the House by 120 to 6 and in the Senate by 60 to 5. Although Minnesota women had been able to vote in school elections since 1876 and in library elections since 1898, the right to vote in all elections had taken them fifty-two long years to achieve. A suffragist described the ensuing scene:

> The moment the Senate vote was polled the corridors, floors and galleries of both houses were in an uproar, hundreds of women cheered and laughed and waved the suffrage colors while in the rotunda a band swung into the strains of the "Battle Hymn of the Republic." ... Mrs. Andreas Ueland, radiant and beautiful as usual, was the center of congratulating men and women. ... "It is my happiest day," she said.

Clara Ueland did not rest on her laurels. Instead, she took the lead in replacing the MWSA with the League of Women Voters, proposed by National American Woman Suffrage Association president Carrie Chapman Catt, as the successor organization to instruct women about the procedures of voting and to involve them in political advocacy. She served only briefly as the first Minnesota League of Women Voters president, resigning that office not only to make way for younger leadership but also to develop a coalition of women's groups to achieve important policy reforms at the state legislature.

Seven years later on a bitter March day, Clara took the long street car ride from the legislature in St. Paul to a stop near her home on Lake Calhoun. As she walked down a hill and began to cross the road to her driveway, a truck, unable to stop on the icy street, hit her. The banner headline across the top of the front page of the *Minneapolis Morning Tribune* told the story, "Mrs. Andreas Ueland Killed."

Despite a blinding snowstorm, 2000 people came to pay homage to Clara Ueland in a public memorial service at the Capitol on March 20, 1927. Visitors will see that she is one of only two women (Dr. Martha Ripley is the other) receiving any kind of recognition in the capitol building for their contributions to the "betterment of the state."

Chambers, Clark A. "Clara Hampson Ueland." In Edward T. James, et al., eds, *Notable American Women, 1607-1950: A Biographical Dictionary.* Vol. 3 Cambridge: Belknap Press of Harvard University Press, 1971.

Minnesota Woman Suffrage Association Records (microfilm edition), Minnesota Historical Society.

Stuhler, Barbara. *Gentle Warriors: Clara Ueland and the Minnesota Struggle for Woman Suffrage.* St. Paul: Minnesota Historical Society Press, 1995.

Ueland, Brenda. "Clara Ueland of Minnesota." 1967. Copy in Minnesota Historical Society.

_____. *Me.* New York: G. P. Putnam's Sons, 1939. Reprints. St. Paul: Schubert Club, 1983. Duluth: Holy Cow Press, 1994.

Nellie Griswold Francis
(1874-1969)

⁕

by Martha Reis and Heidi Bauer

Be it resolved that the Everywoman Suffrage Club of St. Paul, Minn. (Mrs. W.T. Francis, president), does hereby heartily commend the action of this magnanimous body of women, engaged as they are in an effort to uplift all women, without respect to race or color, and wish them unbounded success in this praiseworthy effort to break down the discrimination on account of color.

- Resolution to support the Detroit Federation of Women's Clubs' effort to include the African American Detroit Study Club in the national federation

On October 12, 1914, twenty-five African American women held the charter meeting of the Everywoman Suffrage Club "for the purpose of studying the question of the equal balot [*sic*]." The group elected Nellie Francis as its first president, a post she held until well after the passage of the Nineteenth Amendment in 1920, at which time the club evolved into the Everywoman Progressive Council. The life of Nellie Griswold Francis represents the widely neglected role of African American women in promoting equality in the early twentieth century.

Born in Tennessee in 1874, Nellie Griswold moved with her family to St. Paul in 1883. While a student at St. Paul

High School, Nellie's leadership, rhetorical skills and courage marked the beginning of her career as an activist. The only African American graduate in the Class of 1891, Nellie won honorable mention for a speech entitled "Race Problems." After graduation, Nellie worked as a stenographer at the Great Northern Railway until she married William Trevanne (W. T.) Francis in 1893.

Both Nellie and W. T., a lawyer, were employed in professions generally closed to nonwhites. Nellie Francis went back to work as a stenographer in 1897, working for West Publishing Company until 1907, when her husband's law practice became increasingly successful. This success increased the Francis' involvement in such causes as politics, church and civil duties, racial equality, and women's club activities. After leaving her job at West Publishing Company, Francis was able to devote her full energy to these interests.

While her involvement was widespread, it was as president of the Everywoman Suffrage Club that Francis had perhaps her greatest impact on the political sphere of both Minnesota and the United States as a whole. The Everywoman Suffrage Club was in its very inception linked directly to the suffrage agenda of African American club women at the national level, not as an offshoot of local white women's suffrage groups. In that sense, Francis' involvement contributed to the quest for justice for both her race and gender.

The club, and Francis herself, immediately gained notoriety in the national suffrage movement. Among the guests invited to speak on suffrage at the first meeting was Victoria Clay Haley, visiting Minnesota in her capacity as Assistant Secretary of the National Federation of Afro American Women's Clubs. Francis was a delegate at the 1916 biennial meeting of the National Association of Colored Women's Clubs when that organization urged the submission of the equal suffrage amendment to the constitution. Francis also served as Chair of the Press and Publicity Committee of the National Association of Colored Women's Clubs.

As president of the Everywoman Suffrage Club, Francis

skillfully established a relationship with white woman suffrage organizations in Minneapolis and St. Paul. Such a spirit of cooperation between African American and white women's clubs was by no means a given, and Francis worked for the collaboration of all women's groups across the country. In 1916, she issued a resolution on behalf of the Everywoman Suffrage Club, supporting the decision of the Detroit Federation of Women's Clubs, with only white members, to dissolve affiliation with the national federation unless it extended an invitation to the Detroit Study Club, with only African American members.

Following the victory of the campaign for suffrage, Francis oversaw the transformation of the Everywoman Suffrage Club into the Everywoman Progressive Council. The organization continued to work for "the promotion of political and economic equality and social justice to the Negro, cooperation between white and colored women and men, training of local colored women leaders, and fostering the recognition of Negroes who have achieved success." With the Council, Francis presided over an anti-lynching meeting and worked with state legislators to help pass Minnesota's Anti-Lynching Bill of 1921.

In recognition of her efforts, Francis was honored by her peers with a reception and silver cup, engraved as follows: "Presented to Mrs. Nellie F. Francis by the Colored Citizens of St. Paul for her untiring efforts in behalf of the Race, and in securing passage of the Minnesota Anti-Lynching Bill, April 18, 1921." In her acceptance speech, Francis stated, "Your children will reap the harvest of our solidarity . . . of our determination."

Francis continued her work in Minnesota until 1927, at which time her husband was appointed Minister to Liberia from the United States, the first diplomatic position held by an African American. Liberia had just been granted $50 million in U.S. aid for development, and W. T. was to oversee the project. His work there was short-lived, however. He contracted yellow fever less than a year after his arrival in

Liberia and died in 1929. Upon his death, the U.S. Secretary of State declared that the country had lost "one of its most able and trusted public servants," and the St. Paul City Council passed a resolution detailing his contributions to society, both very unusual actions on behalf of an African American man at the time. Nellie Francis returned to the United States and buried her husband in Nashville, Tennessee. She had retained her family ties in Nashville and lived there for the rest of her life. Francis died in December, 1969, and is buried next to W. T.

"The Anti-Lynching Mass Meeting," *Appeal*, 23 April 1921.

"St. Paul Honors Mrs. W. T. Francis," *Appeal*, 7 May 1921.

Foster, Mary Dillon, ed. *Who's Who Among Minnesota Women*. N.p.: Privately Published, 1924.

Hurd, Ethel Edgerton. *Woman Suffrage in Minnesota: A Record of the Activities in Its Behalf Since 1847*. Minneapolis: Inland Press, 1916.

Jones, Judy Yaeger. "Nellie F. Griswold Francis." In *Women of Minnesota: Biographies and Sources*. St. Paul, Women's History Month, Inc., 1991.

Scott, Anne Firor. "Most Invisible of All: Black Women's Voluntary Associations." *Journal of Southern History* 56 (February 1990).

Stuhler, Barbara. *Gentle Warriors: Clara Ueland and the Minnesota Struggle for Woman Suffrage*. St. Paul: Minnesota Historical Society Press, 1995.

Terborg-Penn, Rosalyn. "African American Women and the Vote: An Overview." In Ann D. Gordon et. al., *African American Women and the Vote, 1837-1965*. Amherst: University of Massachusetts Press, 1997.

"Meeting of Clubwomen," *Twin City Star*, 8 July 1916.

"National Association of Colored Women's Clubs," *Twin City Star*, 20 May 1916.

"Suffrage Club Organized," *Twin City Star*, 16 October 1914.

"Will Represent Minnesota Clubs," *Twin City Star*, 8 July 1916.

"Women's Clubs Convene," *Twin City Star*, 6 July 1912.

"Women's Club for Hughes," *Twin City Star*, 2 September 1916.

"Women's Clubs Take Stand Against Race Prejudice," *Twin City Star*, 15 July 1916.

Elizabeth Hunt Harrison
(1848-1931)

❦

by Barbara Stuhler

*My life has been coexistent with the cause of suffrage
and the League of Women Voters and tremendously
mixed up with them.*

- Elizabeth Hunt Harrison

A remarkably scintillating personality, Elizabeth
Harrison threw herself into civic and church activities with
great enthusiasm and loyalty. She was born Elizabeth Wood
in a parsonage in Chester, New York. She was the third child
and first daughter in the family, an occasion prompting her
father, a Methodist minister, to become a champion of equal
rights for women and men. Born in the year of the first
woman's rights convention in Seneca Falls, New York, reared
in an accepting and expecting environment, and graduated
from Elmira College in 1868, Elizabeth devoted her life to
good works, chief among them the suffrage movement and
the movement's successor organization, the League of
Women Voters.

Elizabeth's second marriage to Hugh G. Harrison, a
Minneapolis businessman and banker, brought her to Min-
nesota in 1877, where she spent the rest of her life. Elizabeth
Harrison was a pillar of the Hennepin Avenue Methodist

Church where, having taught the same Bible class for fifty-two years, she then held the record for the longest Sunday School service in the United States. Her other activities included service as treasurer of the Needle Work Guild of Minneapolis, vice president of the Home for Children and Aged Women, and board member of both the Minneapolis and national YWCA. During World War I, she directed the Red Cross activities of her church.

Most of Harrison's energies, however, went to the suffrage cause. She served as vice president of the Equal Suffrage Association of Minneapolis (later the Hennepin County Woman Suffrage Association) from the time of its formation in 1914 until 1919 when the Minnesota League of Women Voters was formed. She had been an officer of the Political Equality Club of Minneapolis, a member of the Minnesota Woman Suffrage Association, and a member of the Congressional Union, which became the National Woman's Party. She once said, "I know about the adventures, the obloquy, and the thrills attendant on working for the vote, and the joy of seeing an enemy converted into a suffragist."

She gave the Minnesota League of Women Voters the same loyal support and enthusiasm. Harrison was consequently one of six Minnesota women selected for the roll of honor of the National League of Women Voters in 1930. Of the six Minnesotans, three had died—Dr. Ethel Hurd, Maria Sanford, and Clara Ueland; Emily Noyes of St. Paul was too ill to attend the ceremony. There were seventy pioneers honored—women like Susan B. Anthony, Anna Howard Shaw, Carrie Chapman Catt—but only nineteen, including Elizabeth Harrison and Isabel Lawrence of St. Cloud, were present at the ceremony in Kentucky. In her remarks, Harrison noted:

> And now I glory in the League of Women Voters organized for, and accomplishing so much for, the education of the electorate, men and women, and the advancement of mankind. I wish to thank the League of Women Voters in my state and the National League of Women

Voters for putting my name on the roll of honor and making it possible for me to sit this evening with the most distinguished women of the United States of America.

An article in the *Minnesota Woman Voter,* noting the honor to be received by Elizabeth Harrison, expressed some of the reasons for her selection:

> She is never afraid to advocate the causes in which she believes and gives to the League of Women Voters the same enthusiastic support for which she could always be counted during the long suffrage crusade. Her friendliness, her gaiety, her beauty have made her the most popular of champions of unpopular causes and the most agreeable of reformers.

> Mrs. Harrison is a believer in people, in men and in boys and girls as well as in women. She is the center around which a large family converges, the lone star of an innumerable circle of friends, a popular hostess, and a favorite guest, a benefactress as much sought for her sympathy as for her generosity. Heroic in her observance of duty, she counts happiness a duty and radiates it wherever she is.

Harrison died in 1931, living a long and productive life, with much of her time devoted to the rights and advancement of women.

Harrison, Elizabeth. Quoted in *The Minnesota Woman Voter* 10, no. 4 (May 1950): 2.

Foster, Mary Dillon, ed. *Who's Who Among Minnesota Women.* N.p.: Privately Published, 1924.

League of Women Voters Papers, Minnesota Historical Society.

Minnesota Woman Suffrage Association Records (microfilm edition), Minnesota Historical Society.

Anna Dickie Olesen
(1885-1971)

by Marjorie Bingham

*I ask no consideration because I am a woman. I also
ask that no one close his mind against me because I am
a woman.*

> - Anna Dickie Olesen, while campaigning for the
> U.S. Senate

In several ways, Anna Dickie Olesen was the "voice"
of the Minnesota Woman Suffrage Association and of
women's issues in the Democratic Party. She was so well
known for her speaking ability and lively presence that she
joined the Chautauqua lecture series as one of their nationally featured speakers. Though she was concerned with a
variety of social issues, her speeches on woman suffrage reflected the concern over the ratification of the Nineteenth
Amendment. So noted were her abilities that she became the
first woman to be invited to speak at the Jackson Day banquet of the Democratic Party in January 1920. This association with the Democratic Party would lead her to run for the
U.S. Senate in 1922.

Her training ground for such recognition was Cloquet,
Minnesota, where she and her husband Peter Olesen, a school
superintendent, moved in 1908. Anna Dickie had been born

on a farm in Waterville, Minnesota, on July 3, 1885. Her parents, Peter and Margaret Dickie, encouraged her voice training and reading. Her grandmother, Margaret Hughes Davis, was also an influence, telling her how unfortunate it was that women didn't get the vote after all their support in the Civil War. But it was in Cloquet that Olesen's activities in the Woman's Club and her teaching of Americanization classes gained her wider recognition. She served in a variety of positions within the suffrage movement and became vice-president of the Minnesota Federation of Women's Clubs which formed a base of support for her later political activities.

Olesen also acted as a link between the women's organizations and the Democratic Party. She gave a speech in 1916 to the Minnesota Democratic Party State Convention on woman suffrage that "electrified" the event. It also got her onto the Democratic Party's women's advisory committee and in touch with politicians throughout the country. When suffragists celebrated the Minnesota ratification of the Nineteenth Amendment, Olesen was asked to speak. She described the "millions of American women forgetting differences in social conditions . . . religion . . . nationality—we all stand united . . . while all over America there glows a brighter light, and liberty is born anew in the land we love."

With the suffrage campaign over, Olesen used all these links—Chautauqua, women's organizations, and the Democratic Party—to run for the U.S. Senate in 1922. Hard work, including traveling around the state giving speeches wherever she could, won her the Democratic nomination. She campaigned on issues like child labor laws, lower tariffs, and social welfare issues. But she faced two tough opponents in the Republican candidate Frank Kellogg and the Farmer-Labor candidate Henrik Shipstead.

Kellogg had at first taken her candidacy lightly, not returning to Minnesota to campaign. According to historian Dolores DeBower Johnson, he said, "I've got some Swede woman running against me," and he was not worried. But he was told, "That's no Swede woman, that is a Welsh woman and the devil rides her tongue. You'd better go back to Minnesota."

Kellogg did and lost. But it was to Shipstead, not to Olesen. A friend, reflecting on Olesen's defeat, wrote to her that it was probably "too early in the game" for a woman to be elected. Nevertheless, her campaign focused on many women's issues and was nationally reported and watched. As the *New York Globe* stated, "Her candidacy is a wholesome indication of the revival of liberal sentiment and of the growing acceptance of woman in politics."

On a personal level, this high visibility in the Democratic party led her to become state director of the Minnesota National Emergency Council, coordinating state programs for the New Deal. Eventually her family moved to Northfield and it was there she died on May 21, 1971. Though her defeat in the Senate race was difficult to overcome, she nevertheless was the first Minnesota woman who had the courage to take up the "banner" of trying to be elected to a national office. It proved that she practiced what she preached. In 1921, in a message to the Minnesota Women's Club, she had written that "women must not now be laggard in their duties of citizenship." Her all out campaign in 1922 proved that she was no "laggard" herself.

Foster, Mary Dillon, ed. *Who's Who Among Minnesota Women*. N.p.: Privately Published, 1924.

Johnson, Dolores DeBower. "Anna Dickie Olesen: Senate Candidate." In Barbara Stuhler and Gretchen Kreuter, eds., *Women of Minnesota: Selected Biographical Essays*. St. Paul: Minnesota Historical Society, 1977, 1998 revised.

Stuhler, Barbara. *Gentle Warriors: Clara Ueland and the Minnesota Struggle for Woman Suffrage*. St. Paul: Minnesota Historical Society, 1995.

Woman Voter 11 (November 4, 1921): 3.

Bertha Berglin Moller
(1888-Unknown)

by Mary Pruitt

We protest against the 34 willful Senators who have
delayed the political freedom of American women. They
have lined up the Senate with Prussia by denying self-
government to the people.

> - Banner carried by Bertha Berglin Moller, October
> 7, 1918, Capitol Steps

Bertha Berglin was born in Jentland, Sweden, where
women had the right to vote on municipal affairs since 1862.
Two of her uncles, Magnus Ericson and Anders Feanden,
served in the *Riksdag* (the Swedish Parliament) and drafted
legislation for women's rights. Her family came to Minnesota when Bertha was still a child. After attending Rush City
High School and graduating from Duluth Normal School,
she taught school for a few years until she married Charles
Moller in 1910.

Given her roots in the more liberal Scandinavian sys-
tem, and frustrated by the lack of women's political power,
Moller began her career as a political activist in 1916. She
helped organize the woman suffrage campaigns in North
Dakota. When Bertha and Charles Moller moved to Minneapolis in 1918, she volunteered with the Minnesota Scandinavian Woman Suffrage Association. She was also invited

to participate in the Minnesota Woman Suffrage Association (MWSA), and was asked to serve as chair of the state association's congressional committee.

Apparently, the MWSA was not radical enough for her beliefs; in 1918 she devoted her energy to the growing National Woman's Party (NWP), working specifically with the Minnesota Woman's Party (MWP). To dramatize the political struggle for the Nineteenth Amendment, Moller staged suffrage ballets in theaters in Minneapolis, St. Paul, Duluth, and Fargo, North Dakota and Menominee and Milwaukee in Wisconsin. Moller's theatrics focused attention on the NWP's strategy to win suffrage by an amendment to the U.S. Constitution. That was the most radical and direct route in contrast with the state-by-state approach, a time-consuming, if occasionally successful, tactic. In time, however, both radical and moderate suffragists rallied around the federal amendment.

While the performances Moller organized were attracting attention in the Midwest, the NWP had established a picketing campaign initially at the White House and later at the Capitol, but they needed reinforcements. Police had begun a new round of arrests. The hunger strikes and force feedings of the NWP suffragists serving jail sentences continued. Recognizing that the activity in Washington, D.C. was the most direct approach being utilized at the time, Moller headed to the capital. In late August of 1918, *The Suffragist*, the NWP's newsletter, announced "Our Next Demonstration" adding: "Mrs. Charles F. Moller . . . [i]s one of the first women to arrive at headquarters."

In early October, 1918, Moller led marchers to the steps of the U.S. Senate. Brandishing bold new banners, suffragists accused the senators of behaving like Prussians, enemies of the U.S. in the war in Europe. Moller was not surprised at the reaction—she had left home prepared to go to jail. *The Suffragist* reported that police "poured down upon them. . . . They tried to wrench the banners from the women, twisting their wrists and pulling them off the ground." *The Suffragist* photographer captured the scene, with Moller among the leaders of the group. She was arrested eleven times, more frequently than any other Minnesotan.

Moller went to jail twice in 1919 for her participation in the suffrage picketing. Jailed with her were Rhoda Kellogg, Gertrude Murphy, and Sarah Colvin. In January groups of suffragists packed the courtroom for a trial of twenty-three picketers who were accused of lighting paper, oil, wood, and rope for the "Watchfire for Freedom." The women, in essence, took over the courtroom; the judge had difficulty maintaining order, and the bailiff had to drag women to the bench. The women observers in the courtroom applauded for every defendant.

In February, Moller and several others served five days in jail for throwing pine boughs grown in Minnesota onto the "Watchfire for Freedom" in front of the White House. The participants felt that the actual motivation for their arrest was beacuase they burned President Wilson in effigy. Those who were jailed continued their protest with a hunger strike. Moller described the results of their action: "Even those who did not defend the pickets are now indignant at the brutality of the government's methods. And they always go from this to add: 'After all, this delay of [woman] suffrage is inexcusable.'" The actions of Bertha Moller and thousands of suffragists like her helped to shorten that delay.

Moller remained active in politics after the Nineteenth Amendment passed. She was committed to the issue of child labor, and served as publicity director for the National Child Labor Committee. She also was an advocate of the peace movement. In 1921 she enrolled in the University of Minnesota law school. Her rationale for entering law school was "to seek legal equality for women. . . . Until they have equal representation, the chances are they never will receive justice in the courts." When she and her husband moved to Chicago in 1923, she transferred to the law school at Northwestern, but did not graduate. The date and location of her death is not known.

Foster, Mary Dillon, ed. *Who's Who Among Minnesota Women.* N.p.: Privately Published, 1924.

National Woman's Party Papers, Library of Congress.

"Preserving the Dignity of the Court," *The Suffragist*, 25 January 1918.

"Catching Up With Our Allies," *The Suffragist*, 28 February 1918.

"Our Next Demonstration," *The Suffragist*, 31 August 1918.

"Protests Against Willful Senators," *The Suffragist*, 19 October 1918.

"Guilty of —?" *The Suffragist*, 1 February 1919.

"Swedish Women Win Suffrage Before Americans," *The Suffragist*, 7 June 1919.

The Women's Watch. Minneapolis: University of Minnesota's International Women's Rights Action Watch (December 1997).

Victory and Beyond

Marguerite Milton Wells
(1872-1959)

by Barbara Stuhler

> The League exists . . . for the purpose of establishing a
> tradition of responsibility about government.
>
> - Marguerite Milton Wells, on the League of
> Women Voters

Marguerite Milton Wells devoted twenty-seven years
of her life to leadership in the Minnesota Woman Suffrage
Association (MWSA) and in its successor organization, the
League of Women Voters. Born to Nellie Johnson and Edward Payson Wells in Milwaukee, Wisconsin, Marguerite or
"Margie" was reared in the frontier town of Jamestown, North
Dakota, a small treeless community forty miles beyond the
end of the railroad. The experience exposed her to all the
rigors of frontier life and to the process of building a town
and a government. Given the harsh environments of winter
and summer and her interests in outdoor activities, Margie
was permitted to wear boys' clothes and to keep her hair
short. It was not surprising that she persuaded her father to
let her accompany him to an all-male political caucus where
she disguised her sex by wearing a slicker and a cap pulled
down over her bobbed hair. She absorbed the political talk
and reportedly returned home to write all about it—in rhyme!

This precocious youngster, the oldest in a family of one boy and two other girls, entered Smith College in 1891. After graduation, Wells spent time teaching, traveling and joining in a number of organizational good works in Minneapolis where the family had finally settled in 1902. Then in 1917, she marched into the headquarters of the MWSA and offered her services. She was put to work in menial tasks like sorting literature. Clara Ueland, MWSA president, quickly recognized her abilities and assigned her the responsibility of organizing the petition drive that succeeded in generating unanimous support from the Minnesota congressional delegation for the passage of the Nineteenth Amendment. Next, Wells directed the drive for the amendment's ratification, and Minnesota became the fifteenth state to do so.

Meanwhile, Wells attended her first convention of the National American Woman Suffrage Association in 1919 in St. Louis. It was at that convention where national president Carrie Chapman Catt made her historic and eloquent speech proposing as a suffrage legacy the organization of a League of Women Voters to educate newly enfranchised voters. Like other women hearing Catt's words, Wells proved to be an enthusiastic recruit. Some suffrage states, including Minnesota, organized a League of Women Voters even before the Nineteenth Amendment was ratified in 1920.

At its first convention, in October 1919, delegates elected Clara Ueland, MWSA president, to be the Minnesota League of Women Voters president and Marguerite Wells to be First Vice President. Six months later, Clara Ueland resigned (in part to make way for younger leadership), and Wells became president. In 1922 she went on the national board as a regional director. Even as she moved up the ladder of the National League of Women Voters leadership, she maintained the Minnesota League of Women Voters presidency, resigning only when elected national president in 1934. On that occasion, the Minnesota League of Women Voters board members took from Wells' own library her cherished copy of James Madison's *Journal of the Constitutional*

Convention of 1787, had it beautifully rebound and dedicated to Marguerite Wells who "never walks with her back to the wind."

Brenda Ueland, one of Clara Ueland's daughters destined for a career as a writer and iconoclast, described Wells as "a brilliant, slender and charming spinster, high-minded and formidably erudite." Another wrote of her, "When she spoke the effect was compelling. The light, quick voice filled the room; the sentences were terse and simple, but fraught with the power of incisive thinking; the appeal was to energies and motivations that run strongly, always, below the surface of American life."

All of the early League of Women Voters presidents proved to be impressive leaders. Despite Wells' intellectual bent, she believed the League of Women Voters' role in generating individual political action to be its main mission: "Not to amass more knowledge of government, not even to spread it to a greater number of people, but to cause more people to use effectively what knowledge they possess seems today to be the unique aim of the League of Women Voters." In emphasizing individual action as the most effective means whereby the League of Women Voters could make democracy work, she became the architect of the group's philosophy of informed and active citizenship.

Marguerite Wells was one of the younger generation of women who came into the suffrage movement in its final years and who continued to play leadership roles in the League of Women Voters. The last League of Women Voters president with experience as a suffragist, she seized upon the cause of citizen education and advocacy and made it her life's work. She was a small "d" democrat whose insights into the democratic process were lodged in study and analysis. As national president, she was a woman ahead of her time. Much of what she advocated to convert the League of Women Voters into a truly action-oriented organization came to pass after she stepped down from the national presidency in 1944. Marguerite Wells was determined to demonstrate that the suffrage cause was not in vain, and that women, as well as men, could meet the prerequisites of democracy through effective and responsible citizenship.

Cheek, Jeannette Bailey. "Marguerite Milton Wells." In Barbara Scherman and Carol Hurd Green, eds., *Notable American Women: The Modern Period,* Cambridge: Belknap Press of Harvard University Press, 1980.

Stuhler, Barbara. *Gentle Warriors: Clara Ueland and the Minnesota Struggle for Woman Suffrage.* St. Paul: Minnesota Historical Society Press, 1995.

Welles-Wells Family 1636-1936 in the Edward Payson Wells Papers, Minnesota Historical Society Archives.

Wells, Marguerite Milton. "Some Effects of Woman Suffrage," in *Annals of the American Academy of Political and Social Science* (May 1929).

____. *A Portrait of the League of Women Voters.* Washington, D.C.: Overseas Education Fund of the League of Women Voters, 1962.

Young, Louise M. *In the Public Interest: The League of Women Voters 1920-1970.* Westport, Conn.: Greenwood Press, 1989.

Alice Ames Winter
(1865-1944)

---

by Marjorie Bingham

Possibilities loom upon us for great accomplishments.

- Alice Ames Winter, from *The Heritage of Women*

For some, woman suffrage was the goal; for Alice Ames Winter it was a means to an end. While her friend Clara Ueland would take the lead in the persistent drive to get the vote, Winter was showing what could be done with it. Eventually she would be president of the General Federation of Women's Clubs (GFWC), serve on national committees on disarmament and film, and write innumerable articles on education, support for mothers, and women's citizenship rights, among other topics. Throughout all of these activities her driving point was that women should take an active role in the world. She could be quite forceful in her views, as when calling it a "hideous situation" that American women could lose their citizenship by marriage to foreigners and protesting that the U.S. government spent more "on conserving the lives of reindeer . . . than fostering education."

But before her involvement in these national initiatives, Winter began her organizing activities on the local scene in Minneapolis. The daughter of two strong suffrage supporters, Unitarian minister and abolitionist Charles Gordon Ames and the first female factory inspector, Fanny Baker Ames, Alice had been born in Albany, New York, and had spent her childhood in California and Philadelphia. Her education included a B.A. and M.A. from Wellesley College; she taught school in Boston for two years. She came to Minneapolis as the wife of grain trader Thomas Gerald Winter.

As the mother of two, she first became involved in the Minneapolis kindergarten movement. This network of active and socially concerned women formed an early suffrage base. Winter came to support the Minnesota Woman Suffrage Association in a variety of ways. As a founder and first president of the Woman's Club of Minneapolis, Winter urged members to "ally [themselves] with the progressive element" of suffrage. The Women's Club of Minneapolis was not a suffrage organization, however, and several of its members were against the suffrage movement.

After World War I, as former Chair of the Women's Division of the Minnesota Commission on Public Safety, Winter used her networks to rally participation in suffrage activities. An August 30, 1919, letter of hers encourages women to be at the legislative session, "filling the galleries . . . [and] thronging the corridors . . . with energy and optimism and belief in the new day for women."

Winter's activities as the Chair of the Women's Division during World War I were probably the most controversial of her career. The Minnesota Commission on Public Safety has been criticized for discriminatory practices against German-Americans and war critics. Winter was a strong supporter of Americanization programs, but she saw them primarily as a way for immigrant women to participate more fully in American life. She encouraged the Women's Division to work on child care, nutrition, better housing, and citizenship rights alongside their commitment to war work. It was her leadership in these diverse activities that later led her to the presidency of the GFWC.

As president of the GFWC, Winter initiated a building campaign to have a more permanent place and presence in

Washington, D.C. for the organization. Her letters to members supported such progressive measures as the Child Labor Amendment, the Sheppard-Towner Act (mother's aid), an Indian Welfare Committee, and the Women's Joint Congressional Committee. Minnesota's Women's Clubs honored Winter for her national leadership by building a "home demonstration" house in Minneapolis where home economic techniques might be tried, and named it after her. After her term as president of the GFWC, Winter became a contributing editor of *Ladies Home Journal* and later a liaison between women's groups and the film industry to promote more wholesome movies. This connection with the film industry led to a move to Pasadena, California, where she died in 1944.

In addition to her organizational activities, Winter was also a writer of both novels and nonfiction. Though her novels were not critically acclaimed, even there her interests in women's activism came through. In *Prize to the Hardy* for example, the Minnesota female character rescues her male friend, who has a broken leg, by dragging him across a frozen lake in a snowstorm. The image might serve as a theme for Winter's life—women pushing and pulling by use of their own efforts to create better schools, healthier environments, world disarmament and, above all, a place where women could use all their talents. As she wrote in the conclusion of her 1927 book about women's history, ". . . this tapestry of the heritage of women is unfinished."

Chrislock, Carl H. *Watchdog of Loyalty: The Minnesota Commission of Public Safety During World War I.* St. Paul: Minnesota Historical Society Press, 1991.

Houde, Mary Jean. *Reaching Out: A Story of the General Federation of Women's Clubs.* Chicago: Mobium Press, 1989.

Johnson, Dorothy E. "Alice Vivian Ames Winter," in Edward T. James, et. al., eds., *Notable American Women, 1607-1950: A Biographical Dictionary.* 3 vols. Cambridge: Belknap Press of Harvard University Press, 1971.

Ludcke, Jeanette. *You've Come a Long Way, Lady!: The Seventy-Five Year History of the Woman's Club of Minneapolis.* Minneapolis: The Club, 1982.

"Mrs. T. G. Winter Urges Club Women to Support Fees Bill," *Minneapolis Tribune*, 29 November 1920.

Minnesota Woman Suffrage Association Records (microfilm edition), Minnesota Historical Society.

Winter, Alice Ames. *The Heritage of Woman.* New York: Milton, Baleh & Company, 1927.

____. *Prize to the Hardy.* Indianapolis: The Bobbs-Merrill Company, 1905.

Mabeth Hurd Paige
(1870-1961)

by Luella Greene

In 1945 it will be a quarter of a century since we achieved political enfranchisement and in my opinion not nearly enough women are taking part in the country's lawmaking. I had hoped when I entered the legislature in 1923 that by 1943 no less than ten percent of the legislature would be women—yet I am now the only one.

- Mabeth Hurd Paige, in the *Minneapolis Tribune*, March 25, 1944, on her retirement from the Minnesota legislature

Mabeth Hurd Paige was a Minnesota suffrage leader and social reformer who also served as a Minnesota legislator for twenty-two years. In 1949 Paige was among the eight women named as one of the Hundred Living Great Minnesotans by the State Junior Chamber of Commerce at the Centennial Banquet honoring Minnesota's admission as a territory. Paige was not a radical, however. Even though her accomplishments were extraordinary for a woman of her time, she still worked within the constraints of gender, marriage and the upper-middle-class expectations of her family.

Mabeth Hurd was born in Newburyport, Massachusetts, in 1870 to Edward Hurd, a physician, and Elizabeth Sarah Campbell, who was a semi-invalid. As a young girl Mabeth begged to ride along with her father as he drove his horse-drawn buggy to visit his patients. During their conversations, Mabeth declared that she was going to "have a purpose in life even if that meant being an old maid." She also said that she planned to work for the right of women to vote. Her father responded that he hoped that she would remember this, as many women did not "yearn for responsibility in public affairs."

Mabeth's sister, Kate Campbell Hurd Mead, a physician and historian of women in medicine, ended an engagement because her fianceé would not agree to her practicing her profession. But Mabeth agreed to give up her art career for marriage to James Paige, a law professor at the University of Minnesota. While she was in Paris studying, she unexpectedly received an engagement ring. She not only accepted, but agreed to study law since James believed this would make them "completely congenial." He asked that she put his interests first, as most wives at that time were expected to do. They married in June, 1895, and Mabeth Paige began her law studies in September. Paige completed her studies, and, contrary to her husband's wishes, was admitted to the bar. In 1902 their only child, Elizabeth, was born. Paige filled her life with family, church and community activities. She never practiced law.

In 1919, because of her community involvement, Paige was invited by Clara Ueland, president of the Minnesota Woman Suffrage Association, to organize a speaking tour for visiting Canadian suffragist, Nellie McClung. Paige hired a flat-bed truck and arranged a series of open-air street corner meetings for McClung.

When Ueland appointed the Committee on Conference and Organization to establish the Minnesota League of Women Voters in Minnesota, she asked Paige to serve as chair. Paige garnered more than 400 representatives of diverse women's organizations for the two-day planning meeting in October, 1919, where both the bylaws and a constitution were adopted. Paige was also part of the smooth transformation of the National American Woman Suffrage Association into the new and independent nonpartisan National League of Women Voters.

Paige represented the League of Women Voters at a meeting of the Pan-American Conference in Washington, D.C. and returned exhorting women to enter politics. She was then challenged to run for office herself, and agreed to "talk it over with my husband." Somewhat surprisingly, James gave his permission and enthusiastically supported his wife in campaigning for the Minnesota legislature. In fact, he organized a large committee of key men in the district to use in the precinct organization. James had large two-colored campaign posters made and displayed throughout the district. He also visited every hotel and lodging house in the Gateway District on his wife's behalf, since he believed that this was too dangerous for a woman. Mabeth filed as Mrs. James Paige as he requested, but her campaign name was later changed to Mabeth Hurd Paige. Although Paige won by a mere forty-seven votes over her closest challenger, Frank E. Nimocks, she was well prepared when she was elected as a Republican representative from District Thirty (representing the Kenwood area of Minneapolis) in 1922.

In choosing to enter politics, Paige was following the seemingly contradictory directives of Carrie Chapman Catt, founder and first president of the National League of Women Voters. Catt had urged the formation of the nonpartisan league but also said "to make your way there, behind that door . . . [where] the engine that moves the wheels of your party machinery" exists. Paige knew the difficulty of entering this inner sanctum from her experience at national conventions of both parties where she represented the League of Women Voters as Director of Region Five on the National Board.

During her twenty-two year legislative career, Paige also supported many of the same issues that she had as a suffragist and reformer. She served on the Welfare, Education and Public Domain Committees. Paige's legacy included the fifty-four-hour work week for women, establishment of a fourth psychopathic hospital (as hospitals for the mentally ill were then called) at Moose Lake, sewer construction in the Twin Cities to address the problem of pollution of the Mississippi River, environmental protection of Minnesota forests and lakes, and limits on interest on small loans.

After the death of her husband in 1941, and her retirement from the legislature in 1944, Paige returned to volunteer and community work and enjoyed time with her daughter and three granddaughters. Paige died in 1961 at age ninety-one.

Aldrich, Darragh. *Lady in Law: A Biography of Mabeth Hurd Paige.* Chicago: Ralph Fletcher Seymour, 1950.

Flexner, Eleanor. *Century of Struggle: The Woman's Rights Movement in the United States.* Cambridge: Belknap Press of Harvard University Press, 1959; 1971, 1975 revised.

Fraser, Arvonne S. and Sue E. Holbert. "Women in the Minnesota Legislature." In Barbara Stuhler and Gretchen Kreuter, eds., *Women of Minnesota: Selected Biographical Essays.* St. Paul: Minnesota Historical Society Press, 1977, 1998 revised.

James, Edward T., ed. *Notable American Women 1607-1950*, Vol 2. Cambridge: Belknap Press of Harvard University Press, 1975.

Minneapolis Morning Tribune, 25 March 1944.

Minneapolis Sunday Tribune, 20 August 1961. UM Section.

The Minnesota Legislative Manual 1997-98. St. Paul: Election Division, Secretary of State, 1997.

The Minnesota Legislative Manual 1921-22. St. Paul: Election Division, Secretary of State, 1921.

Stuhler, Barbara. *Gentle Warriors: Clara Ueland and the Minnesota Struggle for Woman Suffrage.* St. Paul: Minnesota Historical Society Press, 1995.

Myrtle Cain
(1894-1980)

by Mary Pruitt

. . . no group has ever impressed me so much and I always feel I belong to them even when I do not see or hear from them very often.

- Myrtle Cain to Alice Paul, Chair of the National Woman's Party, 1951

Myrtle Cain was introduced to the cause of woman suffrage at a time when fresh faces and youthful energy were needed to give the movement additional momentum. Born to Irish immigrants and educated at St. Anthony's Convent in Minneapolis, Cain was only in her twenties when she devoted herself to the suffrage movement. After meeting Alice Paul, founder of the National Woman's Party (NWP), Cain became the cofounder of the Minnesota branch, the Minnesota Woman's Party.

The radical militant NWP was the love of Myrtle Cain's political life. Cain marched with Paul and the NWP in one of the nation's first bold suffrage marches. At the march, held in Chicago in 1916, Paul led suffragists in marching backwards against the tide of a much larger patriotic parade—fitting symbolic action for the NWP. The group led the suffrage movement against the cautious, conservative tide, toward a new and radical strategy in the struggle for woman suffrage: to win the vote through an amendment to the U.S. Constitution rather than trying to win the vote state by state.

Ratification of the Nineteenth Amendment provided victory for all suffragists. Once women won the right to vote, many took up the challenge of running for office. In 1922 Cain was elected to the Minnesota House of Representatives as one of the first generation of women legislators. As a legislator, Cain made an impression with two bills: an anti-Ku Klux Klan bill, which passed, and a bill titled "Granting Equal Rights, Privileges and Immunities to Both Sexes," which did not.

The equal rights bill, introduced by Cain and six male colleagues, was adamantly opposed by the other three female legislators as well as prominent Minnesota suffragists like Clara Ueland. Controversy over the bill was a reflection on the division between the NWP and various other women's groups after passage of the Nineteenth Amendment. Some women, including Ueland, felt that an equal rights bill was "too sweeping" and would consequently cause them to lose some of the political ground they fought so hard to gain. The NWP felt that woman suffrage was only the beginning, and that the only way to have equal power was to have equal rights. When the bill on equal rights was introduced to the House, a motion was made to postpone it indefinitely. The motion passed.

Despite the bill's defeat in the state legislature, Cain continued to work in support of equal rights. However, she lost her reelection bid in 1924 by a heartbreaking thirty nine votes. After leaving her elected position, Cain created a life-long career as a political staff assistant, first in the Farmer-Labor Party and then, after the party merger in 1949, in the Democratic Farmer-Labor (DFL) Party. She also worked in the offices of Congressman Roy Wier and U.S. Senator Eugene McCarthy. While her position enabled her to remain active in the political sphere, her feminist politics were circumscribed by the fact that the labor wing of the Farmer-

Labor Party, of which Cain was a founder, did not support the idea of an equal rights bill. Cain had to correspond in secret with Alice Paul about the progress of the fight in Minnesota for equal rights.

Cain remained active on the local front as well, meeting in secret with feminist protégés. From 1948 to 1951 Arvonne Fraser, a political activist, and Myrtle Cain worked together in the DFL office in the Midland Bank Building in Minneapolis. Cain talked to Fraser at length about the drive for woman suffrage and the goals of the NWP, including stories about the brave women who picketed the White House and were arrested and jailed for "obstructing traffic." Cain also acquainted Fraser with the NWP's current bold strategy for change through an equal rights bill. Even though both women could claim greater education and experience than their male counterparts in the DFL office, Cain and Fraser were paid less. They experienced firsthand the need for equal rights.

While initial interest and support eventually waned, by the late 1960s a new wave of feminists "discovered" and publicized the equal rights movement, now identified as the Equal Rights Amendment (ERA). Women's liberationists published newsletters on current events, held conferences on history, and founded college women's studies programs.

Cain had retained her interest on the issue and was able to lend her experience to this new generation of ERA supporters. In 1968 Cain worked as an organizer with Eugene McCarthy's anti-war campaign in Minnesota. That work brought her to the Democratic National Convention in Chicago, where she met a group of young feminists. She spoke to them about the strategies of the NWP and of the future of the equal rights movement. Other young radical feminists studied Cain and the NWP at the socialistic Women's School of Minneapolis. The legalistic women's rights feminists also found in Myrtle Cain a part of their history. Both sides of the modern feminist movement honored Myrtle Cain as a "Founding Mother."

On August 26, 1970, on the fiftieth anniversary of the ratification of the Nineteenth Amendment, the *Minneapolis Star* interviewed Myrtle Cain. The U.S. House of Representatives had passed the ERA but the bill was not then being supported by the U.S. Senate. The opposition to the ERA amused Cain in the *Star* interview: "It's just the same as the opposition they gave the suffrage amendment," she declared. "It's ridiculous that here in the year 1970 we have to eliminate discrimination."

Cain, who never married, was a lifelong activist for the causes that were her passion. She was a member of the League of Catholic Women her whole life, and in her seventies was still active in her support for the ERA. February 12, 1973, was declared Myrtle Cain Day by then Governor Wendell Anderson for her decades of public service. Cain died in 1980, in the home she had lived in most of her adult life.

Myrtle Cain Papers, Minnesota Historical Society.

Chastin, Sue. "Equal Rights For Women Amuse First State Woman Legislator," *Minneapolis Star*, 26 August 1970.

Foster, Mary Dillon, ed. *Who's Who Among Minnesota Women.* N.p.: Privately Published, 1924.

Fraser, Arvonne S., and Sue E. Holbert. "Women in the Minnesota Legislature." In Barbara Stuhler and Gretchen Kreuter, eds., *Women of Minnesota: Selected Biographical Essays.* St. Paul: Minnesota Historical Society Press, 1977, 1998 revised.

LeSueur, Meridel. Interview by Gayla Ellis. Tape Recording. Minneapolis, Minnesota, 1973.

"Contest is Lost for Legislature by Myrtle Cain," *Minneapolis Tribune*, 9 December 1924.

National Woman's Party Papers, Library of Congress.

National Woman's Party Papers, Smithsonian.

Stuhler, Barbara. *Gentle Warriors: Clara Ueland and the Minnesota Struggle for Woman Suffrage.* St. Paul: Minnesota Historical Society Press, 1995.

The Suffragist, 10 June 1916.

Women of Minnesota: Biographies and Sources. St. Paul: Minnesota Women's History Month, Inc., 1991.

Organizations Leading to Woman Suffrage

Abolitionist & Temperance
movements
1830s-1860s

Woman's Rights
Conventions
1848-1861

Equal Rights
Association
1866-1869

American Woman
Suffrage Association
1869

National Woman
Suffrage Association
1869

National American
Woman Suffrage
Association
1890

Congressional
Committee

International Woman's
Suffrage Alliance
1904

Congressional Union
1913

Equality League of
Self Supporting
Women
1907

merge

National
Woman's Party
1916

Woman's Party/
Women's Political Union
1908

League of Women Voters
1919

Developed using information compiled by Marjorie Bingham

Contributors

Sheila Ahlbrand is the associate director of the Upper Midwest Women's History Center. She was a contributor to *Woman's Suffrage in United States History* and was the co-author of *Gender Equity—Past, Present, and Future*, both published by the UMWHC.

Heidi Bauer is the staff editor at the Upper Midwest Women's History Center. She has written for and edited various publications at Hamline University and served as an AmeriCorps volunteer.

Marjorie Bingham has taught history at St. Louis Park Senior High and Hamline University. She is co-author of the *Women in World Cultures* series, one of the founders of the Upper Midwest Women's History Center and wrote the chapter on Minnesota women in *Century of Change*.

Swati Deo is currently studying anthropology and international studies at Macalaster College in St. Paul. She served as an intern at the Upper Midwest Women's History Center for two summers.

Arvonne Fraser is a political and woman's rights activist. She is a former U.S. representative to the United Nations Commission on the Status of Women.

Rhoda Gilman, an editor, researcher, and administrator at the Minnesota Historical Society, has written extensively on upper Midwest history. She was a founder of Women Historians of the Midwest.

Luella Greene carries on Mabeth Hurd Paige's legacy through a dramatic portrayal of her life. Paige is one of 1300 women in *Voices and Images of Women*, Greene's traveling exhibit of women in history.

Lynn McCarthy is a longtime research assistant in the Publication and Research Department at the Minnesota Historical Society. She has also worked for several years as a reference associate in the Minnesota Historical Society reference library and is a history enthusiast and amateur genealogist.

Debbie Miller, research supervisor at the Minnesota Historical Society, is a public historian with special interest in Minnesota, ethnic, and women's history. She collects community cookbooks and excercises her right to vote regularly.

Jane Pejsa is an award-winning writer from Minneapolis. She has published three books, including a biography of Gratia Countryman.

Mary Pruitt is a local historian and professor of women's studies at Minneapolis Community and Technical College.

Martha Reis, a Ph.D. candidate in American Studies and Feminist Studies at the University of Minnesota, is committed to research and writing which make women's history accessible.

Norma Sommerdorf, who lives in St. Paul, has a special interest in historical research and writing, and her articles have appeared in *Ramsey County History* and *Minnesota History*. She is presently writing a story for young people about travel down the Red River trail in 1846.

Barbara Stuhler is the retired executive associate dean of Continuing Education at the University of Minnesota. She is the author of *Gentle Warriors: Clara Ueland and the Minnesota Struggle for Woman Suffrage* and *Ten Men of Minnesota and American Foreign Policy*, and was the co-editor of *Women of Minnesota: Selected Biographical Essays*.

Index

United States Congress (*continued*) Equal Rights Amendment, 164; House of Representatives, 43; opposition to suffrage, 4; Senate, 130, 131; suffrage amendment, 106, 113; suffrage petitions, 69

United States Constitution, 6, 14, 64; suffrage amendment, 106, 136, 162. *See also* Eighteenth Amendment; Fourteenth Amendment; Nineteenth Amendment

University of Michigan, refuses to admit women, 29

University of Minnesota, Board of Regents, 51, 75; Fanny Brin attends, 94; Company Q, 51; Gratia Countryman attends, 50; Equal Suffrage Association, 106-7, 112; Nanny Jaeger attends, 82; Josephine Schain attends, 99; School of Law, Bertha Moller attends, 137; School of Medicine, Ethel Hurd attends, 62; suffrage debate, 99, 100

University of Wisconsin, 87, 89

Washington, D.C., conventions 76; headquarters for General Federation of Women's Clubs, 150-51; suffrage petitions, 69

Watchfire for Freedom, 107, 137

Wellesley College, 150

Wells, Marguerite Milton, *142*, 93, 143-45

White House. *See* Picketing

Wier, Roy, congressman, 162

Willard, Francis, suffrage leader, 39

Wilson, Woodrow, president, 5; burned in effigy, 107, 137; opposes suffrage, 105

Winter, Alice Ames, *148*, 93,

149-51; *Heritage of Women, The*, 149; *Prize to the Hardy*, 151

Wisconsin, opposition to suffrage, 2; suffrage, 106

Wisconsin Alumni in California, 89

Woman's Christian Temperance Union, 13, 44; conventions, 31. See also *Minnesota White Ribbon*

Woman's Club of Minneapolis, 88, 150; Social Economics Department, 88

Woman's Party, 4

Woman's rights, 17, 23, 29, 69, 125, 162; conventions, 1, 25, 123, 166; lectures, 18; legal rights, 38; property rights, 25. *See also* Seneca Falls, N.Y.

Woman's Welfare League, 55, 57

Women's Christian Association, 83

Women's International League for Peace and Freedom, 70

Women's Joint Congressional Committee, 151

Women's Political Union, 166

Women's School of Minneapolis, 163

Women's Trade Union League, 88

Workers' Equal Suffrage Club, 63, 94

World Conference of Food and Agriculture, 101

World War I, 124; relation to suffrage activity, 5, 83, 150

Ypsilanti, Michigan, State Normal School, 30

YWCA, Minneapolis, 124; national, 124; St. Paul, 56